D0933887

JEWELRY
MAKING

JEWELRY MAKING

Hamish Bowie, Hamish

HENRY REGNERY COMPANY · CHICAGO

1977; c.1976   166p

1. Jewelry — Amateurs' manuals *[handwritten]*

© Hamish Bowie 1976. All rights reserved.

First published in New Zealand
and Australia in 1976 by
A. H. & A. W. REED LTD
First published in the United States in 1977 by
Henry Regnery Company
180 North Michigan Avenue, Chicago, Illinois 60601
Printed in the United States of America
Library of Congress Catalog Card Number: 76-6263
International Standard Book Number: 0-8092-8084-1 (cloth)
                  0-8092-7987-8 (paper)

Contents

All dimensions in the illustrations are given in millimetres unless
otherwise indicated

Introduction

Creating a piece of jewellery allows the craftsman to exercise his artistic talents in many ways. The expression given to an object can be either two- or three-dimensional, can involve colour and texture and be inspired by the study of natural form (Illus 1). In the following chapters practical information is given regarding the techniques which may be employed by the craftsman to formulate his own interpretation, and give the created object that touch of individuality.

Many techniques can and should be used to tackle design problems, as rigid approaches tend to give stereotype results. Drawing is probably the most useful way in which to convey ideas quickly, easily and cheaply, although a high degree of skill is required to draw in a meaningful way. This can be acquired with practice. One of the best ways is to go out with a sketch pad and draw interesting forms. Use a B or 2B pencil, sharpen it to a wedge point, and experiment, creating lines of differing thicknesses and using the broad edge of the wedge for creating shadows and tones. Select objects which will help when drawing jewellery such as elipses. These are used when drawing rings, and are one of the more difficult forms to express because of their three-dimensional character. It is important to master this. Practise constructing them within a box (Illus 2); sketch jam-jars, teacups, anything that has an elipse, drawing them freely, smoothly moving the arm from the elbow in sweeping arcs. To learn more about sketching textures and form use a magnifying glass on such things as the bark of a tree, or a section through a cabbage or seed pod.

The designer first and foremost has to be a creator and problem solver. It is difficult to start designing without first drawing up a brief or guide lines around which ideas can evolve. One of the best approaches is to select a particular section of material with which to work. Thin copper wire is very suitable as it can be easily

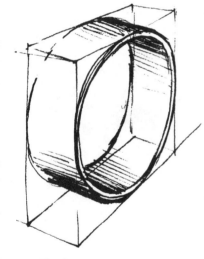

Illus 2

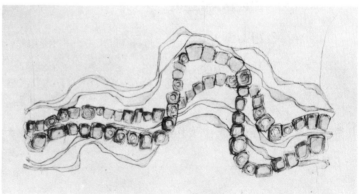

Illus 1 Necklace derived from a corn cob designed by Stephanie Smith

6

manipulated around mandrels and pliers. Try coiling it to produce rings of different diameters and place these together to form patterns and combinations which might, for instance, make a brooch or a unit for a linked bracelet or necklet. Develop the results by introducing wire of differing sections, sections of tube and pieces of sheet metal (Illus 3).

To involve colour in these simple constructions beads, stones, enamels, or resins can be used. In simple wire jewellery beads can be glued or threaded on. Colour is an important consideration and today the jeweller has an infinite variety of materials at his disposal each presenting colour in one form or another, eg Titanium, acrylics, resins, bone, ivory, ebony, shell, varieties of wood, enamels, and of course, stones.

To make a design from which to work potato prints on paper may be made to represent areas of colour and is an ideal technique for reproducing the shape of a unit many times (Illus 4). Stencils simply cut from card are also suitable for this purpose. Paint may be applied to represent metal or stones and for this watercolours are very suitable. To represent yellow gold use a thin wash of mid-chrome yellow with a touch of burnt sienna, and neutral tint or peynes grey mixed in to give the required tone. Thin washes on white paper, leaving highlights unpainted, can be very effective but must not be laboured. Silver may be represented on white paper using a thin wash of peynes grey, again leaving the highlights unpainted to simulate reflective points. Stones can be represented with washes of colour, highlighted with white paint on

Illus 3   Sketch by Stephanie Smith to develop ideas for the use of wire and other pieces of metal

Illus 4   Repeated unit design by Stephanie Smith achieved by using potato print and outlining with a pen

reflective areas, and neutral tint (or peynes grey) to distinguish shadow areas. A stone is a three-dimensional object and should be treated as such.

With any representational work the direction of the light striking the object must always be considered so that the areas of reflection and shadow can be determined and treated in the appropriate way. Edges and corners can be highlighted with white paint, the shadow edges with a dark line. Metal may be treated in this rather harsh manner for unlike other materials it has a highly reflective surface which tends to have linear qualities in the transition from reflection to shadow. Illus 5 shows a painted representation of a pendant and chain. Pieces of coloured paper can be glued on to represent enamelled areas or coloured stones, but tinsel, paste stones, or coloured beads, may also be applied in this way to represent areas of colour.

Illus 6 shows a design made by using ordinary household objects. It is only a short step from these simple ideas to an interpretation in metal with stones etc.

Illus 6   Design by Stephanie Smith for a pendant made by an arrangement of elastic bands on wire glued to card

1 Basic Techniques

The main skills of any metalsmith whether working with gold or tin, are hammering, filing, saw piercing, and soldering. It is important to understand how the metal can be controlled and manipulated. It is quite amazing what can be achieved by a beginner with the simplest tools. With hammers, for example, a piece of sheet metal can be raised into bowl forms; smooth flat areas and great varieties of textures can be achieved; and the metal distorted into shapes far removed from its original form.

Hammering

Hammering, or forging, is one of the first techniques to explore (Illus 7) as very little equipment is required. For most operations hammers and a hefty engineer's vice bolted to a sturdy bench are

Illus 7
Cross pene
raising hammer

Illus 7b
planishing
hammer

Illus 8

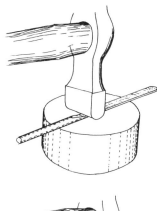

Illus 9 The direction in which the cross pene raising hammer is used has a considerable effect on the reaction of the metal. Hammering in the direction shown above causes the metal to flatten and elongate; hammering in the direction shown below causes the metal to flatten and broaden

Illus 10 The wire is approximately 1mm in diameter. Cut four lengths and flatten with the ball of the ball pene hammer where required against a flat stake in the vice. A loop is turned on the end of each length. A cross piece (a) is made from slightly thinner wire and a loop turned on one end. Four spacers are cut from tubing which will fit over the cross piece. All the components are polished and threaded onto the cross piece in the correct order. The other end of the cross piece is turned into a loop

essential. A steel block clamped into the vice (Illus 8) gives a horizontal working surface which should be smooth and free from pitting. If the surface is bad it must be filed back and smoothed off with varying grades of emery paper until a fine even finish is achieved.

Experiments with hammers on copper wire can produce interesting shapes which may be employed to form a piece of jewellery. The object of the exercise, however, is to obtain, through experience, an understanding of how to control the metal (Illus 9). It is possible then to go on to produce simple forms which can be made into items of jewellery (Illus 10). Before doing this it would be helpful to make a Plasticine model to follow. Plasticine moves and moulds in much the same way as metal and can be cut and shaped to sections resembling the metal before forging. It can then be pushed and moulded to sections similar to those produced after forging. Textures and details can all be worked on the surface with knives and by making impressions with various objects. Illus 11 and 12 show the progression from simple forms to more controlled work and the finished piece.

To extend the possibilities of forging it is necessary to buy one or two stakes – shaped implements on which metal can be formed. One of the most important is a small *anvil*. This is probably the most versatile piece of equipment having a circular tapered end, a square tapered end, and a flat bit in the middle. One end can be used for forging flat areas such as in square settings, and the other for circles such as in round settings or rings which require textur-

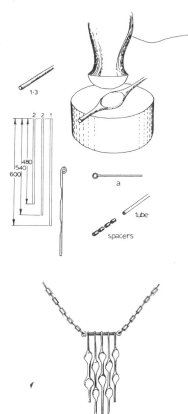

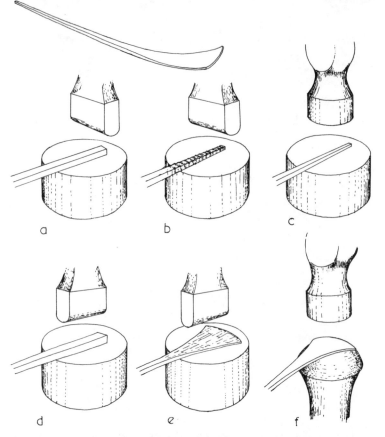

Illus 11 Forging experiment using a cross pene raising hammer and a flat planishing hammer. The stake used for the first five stages is a flat stake: the final stage forms a spoon shape over a domed stake. a and b the square rod of copper is forged equally on each side with the cross pene raising hammer until the required taper is achieved; c the surfaces are trued and smoothed with a flat planishing hammer; d and e the other end of the rod is worked with the cross pene raising hammer to flatten it; f the flattened end is worked over a domed stake with a flat planishing hammer to form a spoon shape

ing with punches or a hammer (Illus 13). Certain domed stakes are useful for forging and forming spoon shapes (see Illus 11) – see also the sections on doming and raising metal in Chapter 2.

At this point I would like to make it clear how important it is that all tools are kept in good condition. Hammer faces should be polished and the edges of the flat surfaces gently rounded off. This is often ignored by beginners so that a great deal of work is necessary at a later stage using files and emery paper to remove the blemishes from the hammered metal, destroying the finish. Part of the beauty of hand-forged work is the finish imparted by a properly hammered surface. Illus 14 shows a bracelet constructed from forged pieces of gold.

To thicken a piece of metal it has to be supported firmly in the vice with protective copper plates on the jaws grasping and holding the metal as close to the area being thickened as possible. The metal is then beaten back onto itself so expanding the section (Illus 15). This technique is often used to form the ends of a forged wire neckband.

During all hammering operations the metal must be annealed to prevent it cracking (see Chapter 3).

Texturing

Forging produces a particular sculptural effect to which various textures can be applied. These are done by using hammers alone,

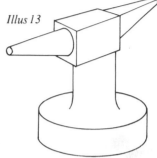

Illus 12 A necklet forged from silver wire set with an agate rose, designed and made by Sylvia Gray

Illus 13

Illus 14 9ct gold bracelet designed and made by Hamish Bowie

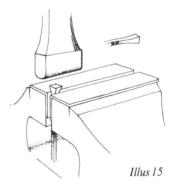

Illus 15

or in conjunction with other implements. Texture can also be created by heating metal until it is on the point of melting. If this is carried out carefully the metal will shrivel and produce interesting effects but a great deal of control is required otherwise the metal will melt into a blob.

Each hammer edge produces a different result. For example the edge of a *cross pene hammer* which has either been gently rounded off or sharpened to a fine edge as in Illus 16, can produce one sort of texture, and the ball of a *ball pene hammer* is used for a gentle texture, consisting of small indentations. But whatever technique is applied, it is essential that the metal being worked is supported properly either on a steel block or in pitch as described on page 36.

Another way of texturing is with *punches*. These have to be made of tool or silver steel which can be bought in its soft unhardened state in standard dimensions. The steel should be cut into lengths of about four inches and filed into pointed ends or broad

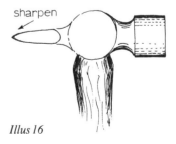

Illus 16

ends on which criss-cross patterns can be cut with *saws* and *needle files*. Textures can also be imprinted by bringing the punch to a red heat and beating the broad end on a roughened surface, such as a coarse file.

Once the pattern is made the punch has to be hardened and tempered so that it will withstand a lot of use. This is done by bringing it to a red heat (not white heat which will spoil the steel) and immediately quenching it in a bucket of cold water. This will harden the steel but leave it so brittle that a hammer blow would shatter it. To temper, or soften the steel to a point where it will not shatter but will be hard enough to withstand the hammer, the black oxide left by the heating and hardening process has to be removed with emery paper. The bright metal is exposed along one side of the punch and is smeared with oil. The punch is then held in a pair of tongs and the end gradually heated. As the temperature increases the metal will change colour through shades of yellow. When it turns browny-yellow it should be quenched immediately in a bucket of cold water. Over a period of time a collection of punches can be built up and these are a valuable asset to any jeweller.

The punches are used in the following manner: the object to be textured is supported against a steel block held in the vice (Illus

Illus 17

17). Strike the punch with a hammer, move the punch to the next position and strike it again. Alternatively the object may be set in a pitch bowl as described for chasing (page 36).

Circular cutting punches can be bought or made. They are useful for producing textures, but may also be used for cutting discs out of thin sheet metal approximately 0.4mm thick. They are made from a length of steel in the soft state. Firstly a recess is machined or drilled in one end, then the edge is sharpened to a bevel around the circumference (Illus 18). The punch should then be hardened and tempered. When using these punches to cut through thin sheet metal it is important that the metal is supported on a soft material such as wood, copper, or lead, to protect the sharp edge.

A *pendant drilling machine* with flexible drive (Illus 19) and tiny dentist's drilling burrs (Illus 20) can also be used for texturing. Some skill is required in controlling the drill but with a little practice an amazing variety of surfaces can be achieved. Gentle brushed textures can be created by light application and a gentle backward and forward movement, or a bark like surface can be achieved with deep gouges. Care should be taken when approaching the edges of the metal with the rotating burr because if it is rotating in a direction where it will bite into the edge it can easily dig in and damage the work, and craftsman (Illus 21).

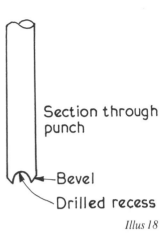

Section through punch

Bevel

Drilled recess

Illus 18

Illus 19   *Illus 20*

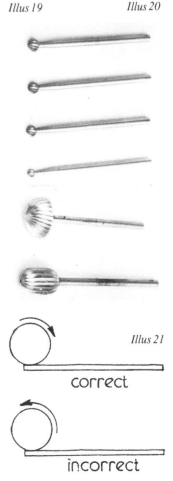

Illus 21

correct

incorrect

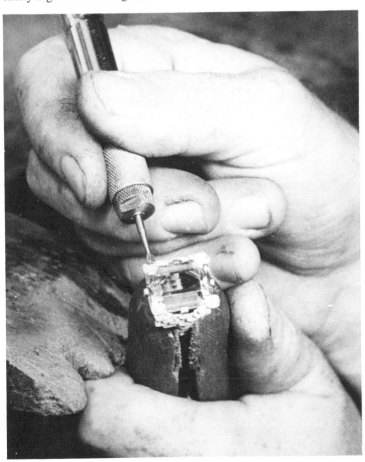

Filing

Having produced one or two interesting forms and textured them, certain areas may need to be smoothed and polished. The smoothing is done with files and various grades of emery or sand-paper. The files in Illus 22 will cover most requirements for large work. Illus 23 and 24 show small needle, *escapement*, and *riffles files* which are used for more intricate work.

Before beginning work it is very important that the metal should be held and supported properly, either in the hand against the bench, or in the vice with protective copper plates on the jaws (Illus 25). Although work can be done on the kitchen table it is better to buy or adapt a bench to the specification shown in Illus 26. This consists of a cut out area enabling the work to be carried out more easily, and a skin or tin tray fastened across the gap to catch the filings. The replaceable hardwood peg is very useful for supporting metal pieces when they are being filed.

The important rules to remember about filing are always to use

Illus 22 Two half round and two flat large jeweller's hand files. These files are three times the size of those shown in *Illus 23*

the broadest file possible as smaller ones give an irregular finish; never concentrate on one spot but work over the entire surface evenly and gradually, so that it is all finished at the same time; always work across the direction of previous filing operations so that the rough marks are erased by smoother ones. The file only cuts when it is being pushed forward, so if you are a beginner, remember to lift the file at the end of each stroke and do not drag it back over the metal. If there is a lot of material to remove from the work, begin with a *No 2 rough cut file* and progress to the smoother files as the contour required is achieved.

Cylindrical objects such as rings should be firmly supported by a notch in the bench peg. When filing the internal radius start with the largest size *half round file* that will comfortably fit, and operate the file with a forward twisting action of the wrist. This is very important as it ensures even working by causing the file to cover a wider area than in normal straight pushes. For the outer surfaces, much the same applies. The movement of the wrist ensures that the flat surface of the file will follow the round contour of the metal.

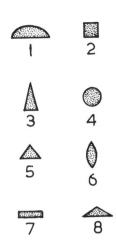

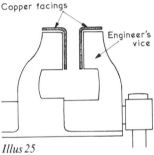

Illus 24 Needle file shapes: 1 half round; 2 square; 3 knife edge; 4 round; 5 three square; 6 double half round; 7 parallel flat; 8 triangular with cut on the one broad face only

Illus 25

Illus 23 Riffle files (bottom) and needle files (top)

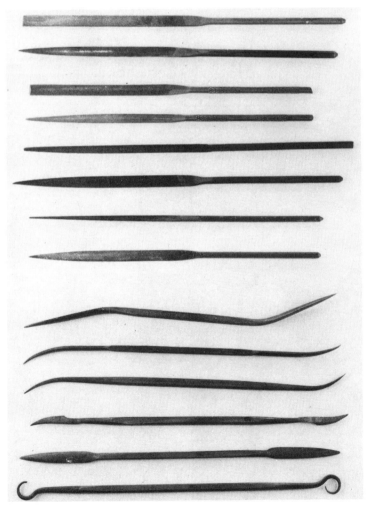

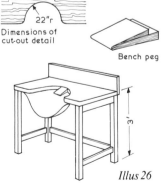

Illus 26

17

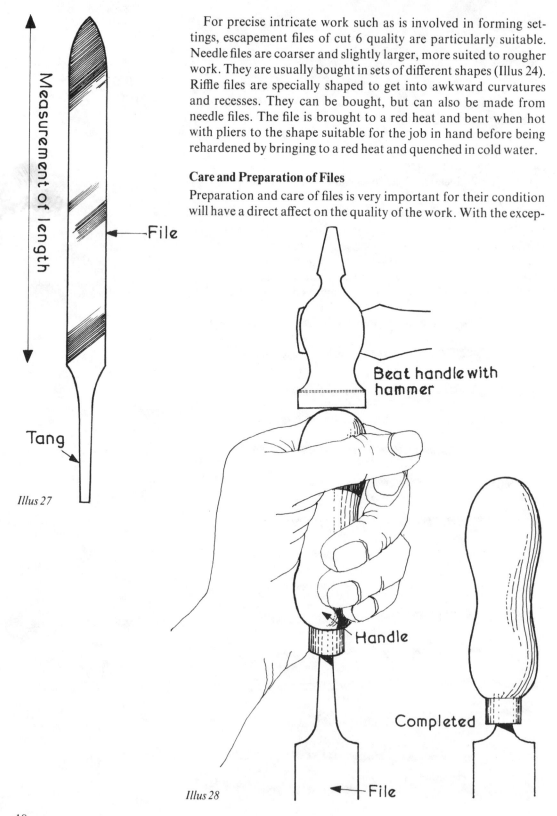

For precise intricate work such as is involved in forming settings, escapement files of cut 6 quality are particularly suitable. Needle files are coarser and slightly larger, more suited to rougher work. They are usually bought in sets of different shapes (Illus 24). Riffle files are specially shaped to get into awkward curvatures and recesses. They can be bought, but can also be made from needle files. The file is brought to a red heat and bent when hot with pliers to the shape suitable for the job in hand before being rehardened by bringing to a red heat and quenched in cold water.

Care and Preparation of Files

Preparation and care of files is very important for their condition will have a direct affect on the quality of the work. With the excep-

Measurement of length

File

Tang

Illus 27

Beat handle with hammer

Handle

Completed

Illus 28

File

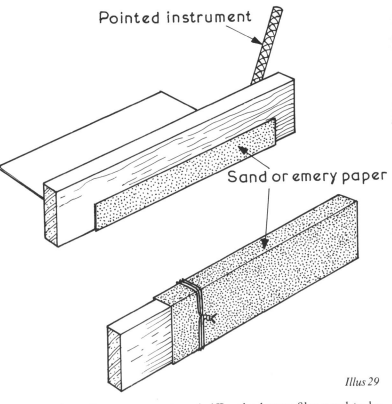

Pointed instrument

Sand or emery paper

Illus 29

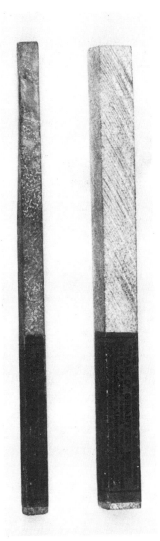

Illus 30

tion of needle, escapement, and riffle, the larger files need to be tempered, the roughness removed, and handles fitted on. To temper a file it is held tip downwards in a pair of tongs and dipped into turpentine. It is then set alight and allowed to burn out, so tempering the surface, which is normally too hard and brittle for the soft metals used by jewellers. This process also reduces the risk of the teeth of the file being chipped out with use. The next procedure is to rub all of the working surfaces with chalk to reduce clogging. A special wire brush is used to clear files if they do get clogged. Appropriate handles must be fitted to the files so that they can be controlled properly. There are two parts to a file, the blade and the tang and all measurements given refer to the blade only (Illus 27). The soft unhardened pointed end, or tang is brought to a red heat. Care should be taken that the heat is restricted to the tang otherwise the file will be spoilt. The handle is forced onto the tang initially by hand pressure, and then by holding the handle and beating the end with a hammer (Illus 28). The file should not be rested against anything during this operation but rely solely on the shock of the hammer blows to force the handle over the tang. When the files are not in use make sure they do not rub against each other as this causes damage. Needle files can be stood in a block of wood with holes drilled in it. The larger files should be held in clips or by loops. Such care will appreciably extend their life span.

When work with all the files has been completed more rubbing is done with various grades of emery or sandpaper. As for filing, the metal must be held firmly either against the bench peg or in the vice. Another important rule is that the emery paper should be fastened to a piece of wood to form a buff stick. To improvise this wrap the paper round a lathe of wood 300 × 35 × 6mm. Place the paper face down on a board and use a sharp point to score a line down its length about 12mm from the edge. It is then folded at right angles along the score and the lathe of wood placed into the right angle. A score is made against the other side of the wood and the paper folded and drawn tightly round the wood (Illus 29). This process is continued until all the paper is tightly wound onto the lathe and then bound with a piece of wire. As the buffing surface becomes worn it can be ripped off and a fresh one exposed.

Initial work should be carried out with coarse paper grade 2, going on to grade 1, and finally grade 0, which will give a fine surface suitable for polishing. However if it is important to retain a very flat surface with crisp edges further work can be carried out with finer grades down to 4/0. This will make the process more gradual and achieve a surface requiring less work at the polishing stage when edges can easily be rounded off.

Another very excellent smoothing agent is *Water of Ayre Stone* or *Scotch Stone* (Illus 30). This is available in a variety of sizes but generally only the 6 and 12mm square are necessary. The stone is used with water as a wetting agent to give a fine matt surface suitable for polishing, and is particularly good when working in close proximity to stones which normally would be damaged by emery. Water of Ayre can be shaped with the file so that it will fit into awkward corners. Again, work across the direction of previous work in straight lines, never with circular action.

Polishing

Polishing is most important because poor finishing can spoil an otherwise excellent piece of work. It can be done by hand or with an electric polishing lathe but there is no doubt that the mechanical method is quicker and produces a superior finish, although it takes longer to master. Polishing should be a short process, removing only a small amount of metal without distorting shape or rounding off corners, and should only be done after filing followed by preparation with emery paper has been thoroughly carried out.

Whichever technique is used certain polishing agents are necessary: a bar of tripoli, a bar of rouge AA quality, and a pound of pumice powder for hand finishing. For polishing by hand, mix the pumice with light machine oil to form a smooth paste and apply this to a strip of chamois leather glued to the flat surface of a wooden lathe (Illus 31). Start rubbing at right angles to previous work, until an even matt surface is achieved. With a soft brush clean the object in hot water with liquid detergent and ammonia to remove traces of the polishing media which must not be carried

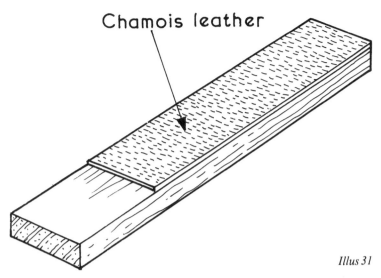

Chamois leather

Illus 31

over to the next stage. Then tripoli dipped in turpentine is applied to a fresh strip of chamois and again the work is polished at right angles to previous work. By now the surface should be semi-polished, requiring only final brightening after careful cleaning. This is carried out with a mixture of rouge and turps on another chamois strip and is achieved by working across the direction of previous work with light movements.

A polishing lathe is simply an electric motor with a spindle which has tapered ends on which there is a coarse thread. If you can afford one buy a motor of at least $\frac{1}{4}$ horse power. The motor should be able to run at a constant speed under load, anything less powerful will slow down when in use which is very undesirable. Polishing mops of calico, about 100mm diameter and 37mm wide are required, and it is necessary to have at least two of these – one for each grade of polishing composition – as it is important that the compositions are kept separate for a trace of one will spoil the effect of another. The calico mops screw on to the spindle and if you have a double-ended motor you can keep one side for rouge and the other for tripoli.

Before beginning, the mops have to be prepared. Run the motor with the fresh mops on and apply a piece of coke or cheese grater heavily to the perimeter several times (Illus 32). This causes the material to fray and the surface become soft. The threads which stand up from the surface must then be removed, for they will actually scratch the surface of the metal during polishing. This is done by careful singeing over an open flame. Go round a little way at a time ensuring that any smouldering is extinguished when the offending threads have gone by pressing the mop into the palm of the hand for half a second, several times. This must be done quickly to avoid burning yourself. Small areas can be gripped quickly between finger and thumb. Make sure the mop is not smouldering when you put it back on the motor for it will go up in a ball of flame and be completely ruined. Do *not* wet the mop. Illus

Illus 32

33 shows a rouge mop prepared in this way, a stick of rouge composition and a mop before preparation.

The mops should now have an even surface and feel soft and downy to the touch. They are ready for the polishing agents which are applied as they revolve. Start with tripoli which may be dampened in turpentine prior to application. A tripoli mop with a bar of tripoli is shown in Illus 34. Work across the direction of the previous emery buffed finish initially and as the marks are crossed out move the object to change direction so as to produce an even surface. Take care not to work too long in one direction. The surface should be even, free from ripples or traces of emery buffing and have a semi-polished appearance. When polishing remember always to go over the edges, never into them, otherwise at the very least you will round them off, if not have a severe accident caused by the mop catching the edge and tearing the object from your hands and hurling it at high speed in any direction – even back at you! Hold the object tightly if it is a flat sheet or support a length of wire on a piece of wood (Illus 35).

Once a satisfactory finish is achieved with tripoli the next stage is rouge polishing. This is carried out after the object has been thoroughly cleaned as described for hand finishing and gives the

Illus 33

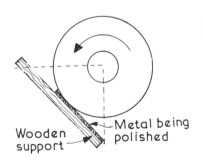

Illus 34

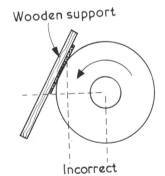

Wooden support

Incorrect

Wooden support

Metal being polished

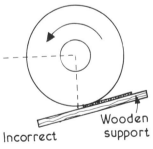

Incorrect

Wooden support

Illus 35

final high polish. You can use a composition rouge which has a binding wax, or AA quality stick rouge – a hard dry compressed bar (Illus 33). Composition rouge is less dusty and does not fly about as much as the bar which needs to be wetted with turps before being applied to the mop. The rouge is also applied to the mop when it is revolving. When you come to the last finishing stage use turps with either type of rouge to act as a fine lubricant to give that final glisten. Work across the direction of previous stages as before. Another point to remember is that as the polishing operation progresses the pressure between the metal and the mop should be reduced until in the end you are just feathering the surface and changing the direction frequently. Rouge polishing is shown in Illus 36.

Besides the calico mops there are various felt bobs which can be used (Illus 37). For flat surfaces a 100mm diameter by 25mm felt mop is very useful. Either the edge or the flat side may be used depending on the surface being polished. Tripoli is applied to the felt whilst it is revolving and the metal, which should have been prepared with emery, held against it. The object can then be

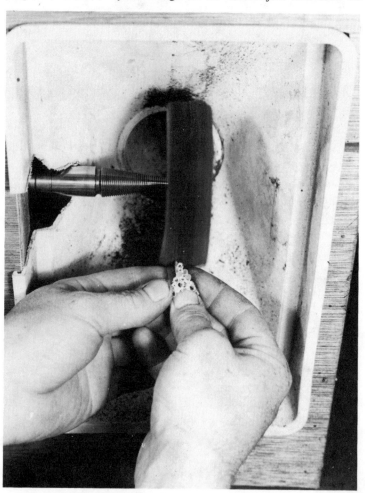

Illus 36

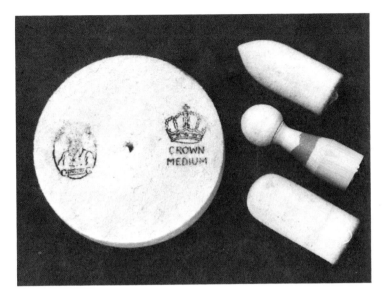

polished in the usual way. The tapered finger felt (Illus 37) is used on the lathe for preparing the insides of rings after emery buffing. For final polishing run cotton wool onto the tapered ends of the polishing motor. This will form a soft finger mop suitable for rouge polishing with the aid of a little turps. The surface of the felt clogs and from time to time has to be renewed. This can be carried out while the spindle is running using an old file to scrape away the old part.

The polishing of wire and intricate textured surfaces can be carried out using either bristle or brass wire brushes attached to the lathe (Illus 38). With the bristle brushes use tripoli or rouge and turpentine. With the brass brush use a solution of water and detergent only. This is called scratch brushing and it is essential that it is carried out wet, either by dipping the metal in the solution from time to time, or, better still, rigging up a slow drip feed onto the brush as it revolves (Illus 39). The wire object must be supported on a piece of wood before coming into contact with the brush. At

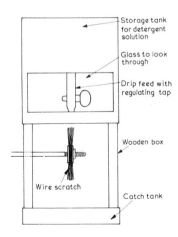

Storage tank for detergent solution

Glass to look through

Drip feed with regulating tap

Wooden box

Wire scratch

Catch tank

Illus 39

25

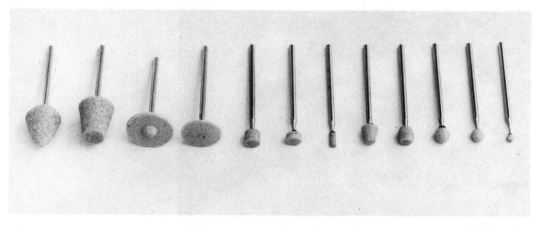

Illus 40

Illus 41

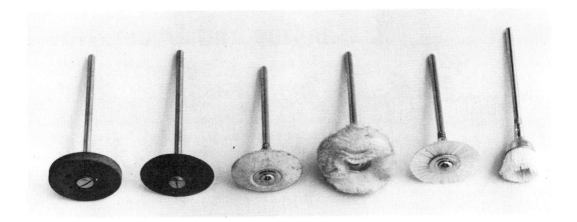

Illus 42

no time should it be held to the mop without support, for it is liable to be torn from your hand and ruined.

Excessive solder and marks in awkward places can be ground with small grindstones (Illus 40) and the parts smoothed with emery impregnated rubber wheels, which come in a variety of shapes (Illus 41), then polished with a flexible shaft using tiny polishing mops, brushes, or felts (Illus 42). The procedure is exactly the same as for the large mops on the lathe. But as it is always preferable to use as large a polishing area as possible, tiny mops are seldom used. For example a sheet of metal 50mm square should be polished with a mop at least 100mm in diameter. Polishing with a small 12mm diameter mop would produce an irregular totally unsatisfactory surface. Certain awkward areas can be polished using threads, string or tape. The procedure is to hook the material around a nail in the bench, apply either tripoli or rouge, pull the material taut and rub the object to be polished on its surface. The threads may be passed through and around things to polish areas that normally would be very difficult to finish. These threads are available from suppliers of polishing materials.

2 Shaping and Decorating

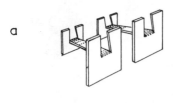

a

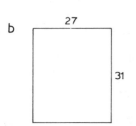

b

27

31

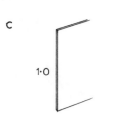

c

1·0

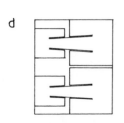

d

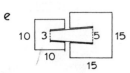

e

10 | 3 | 5 | 15

10

15

f

Illus 43   Pair of cufflinks; a finished cufflinks; b sheet of metal; c thickness; d pierce cufflinks out with jeweller's saw-frame; e bend at the dotted lines; f the finished items may be polished or textured as required

As your capabilities as a craftsman improve, you will wish to experiment with new techniques. Working with sheet metal involves a great many skills, and to help master these there is a wide range of implements. Initially, it is important to discover what can be done with sheet metal, and it is often a good plan to work out designs in cartridge paper. This can be bent, cut, and handled in much the same way that the metal is manipulated. To begin with I suggest trying simple jewellery pierced and folded from sheet metal (Illus 43, 44, 45, 46). You can then experiment with textures and variations on these ideas. On a piece of scrap metal experiment with effects produced by dental burrs and texture punches to find out what is suitable for the object being made.

Saw Piercing

One of the most important techniques to master is saw piercing. This is done with a jeweller's saw frame and blade which are available in a range of thicknesses and sold in bundles of a dozen of any one size (Illus 47). For the average saw piercing work a blade of No 1 thickness is suitable, and this is fastened into the frame under tension as in Illus 48 with the teeth facing backwards towards the handle. Before piercing it is important to have a suitable surface for working on, and it is essential to ensure that the metal can be supported firmly. Although a great deal of work can be done on the bench peg, it is advisable, if there is a lot of piercing to be done, to make a special support. This can be done with a lathe of wood approximately 10mm thick by 75mm wide fastened to the bench and positioned across the cut out (Illus 49). In the centre of the front edge a V-shape cut is made for the saw to work in.

Illus 44   Simple cufflinks designed and made by Hamish Bowie

28

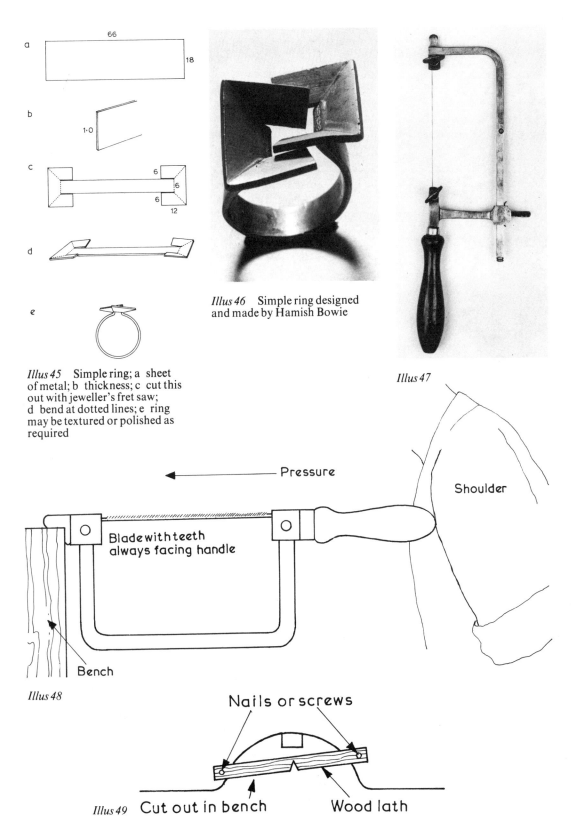

a

66

18

b

1·0

c

6

6

6

12

d

e

Illus 46 Simple ring designed and made by Hamish Bowie

Illus 45 Simple ring; a sheet of metal; b thickness; c cut this out with jeweller's fret saw; d bend at dotted lines; e ring may be textured or polished as required

Illus 47

Pressure

Shoulder

Blade with teeth always facing handle

Bench

Illus 48

Nails or screws

Cut out in bench

Wood lath

Illus 49

29

The best sheet metal to work with is copper or gilding metal of between 0.7mm and 1.0mm thick (the latter is easier to pierce as it is harder and less liable to bend or clog the saw blade). A disc is marked out with a pair of springbow type dividers (Illus 50) and the metal placed flat on the lathe of wood. The saw frame is held as in Illus 51 and moved up and down using the full length of the blade. It should work vertically. Never operate it at an angle but turn the metal keeping the blade working within the V cut. When following the line marked on the sheet, always make sure that the blade cuts outside of that line. If the blade runs down the centre of the line the disc will be undersize. Ideally the line should remain visible so that the final truing and finishing of the edge can be carried out with a file. If the saw blade jams and binds it is advisable to rub it with beeswax or candle wax which acts as a lubricant.

Forming

Once a disc has been cut with the saw it can be made into different forms. The simplest one is a single curvature, but even this requires the use of *forming tools*. These are devices generally consist-

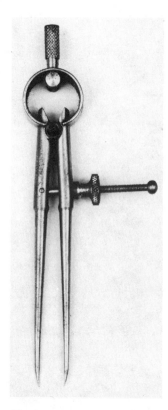

Illus 50

Illus 51

30

ing of male and female parts in steel or hardwood. The male is used to force the disc into the contour of the female. Steel formers (Illus 52) can be bought but are expensive. You can make wooden ones from beech, oak, mahogany, boxwood, or dowel which is very suitable for the male tool (for the larger curvatures use a piece of broomstick). The female former must be cut from hardwood with a saw and finished with a coarse file then sandpapered to exactly the same shape as the disc is to take. The metal is placed in the curvature of the female former and the male former pressed down onto it, gently at first, with an action like a rolling pin, so that the metal bends evenly into form (Illus 53). Hand pressure and the rolling action will almost complete the operation, but it is necessary to finish the process by tapping the male former with either a hide or wooden mallet. During the operation move the metal disc backwards and forwards in the former so that an even contour is achieved.

It is important, as in all forming operations, that the surface of the metal being worked is free from any deep marks and has been prepared to at least a fine emery finish. The forming implements should also be well finished with fine sandpaper, as any defect will

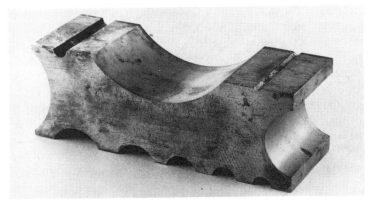

Illus 52

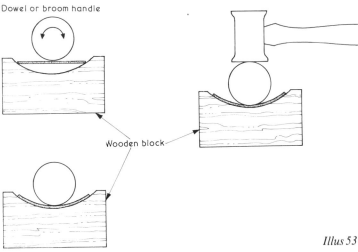

Illus 53

be transferred to the metal and be awkward to remove afterwards.

The disc can also be made into a dome shape using a sand bag (a circular leather cushion filled with sand) and a round faced wooden mallet (Illus 54). An indentation is pressed into the sandbag with the wooden mallet. The disc is then placed in the indentation and carefully beaten with the mallet (Illus 55). To ensure an even contour, rotate the disc as it is being beaten so that the whole surface is subjected to the same treatment.

To dome or dish metal shapes which are not geometric use a block of lead and polished steel doming punches like the ones in Illus 56. A variety of sizes are necessary because the work is begun with large diameter punches and carried on down the smaller punches till the required contour is achieved. The technique is to beat an impression into the lead block using a punch and a 4oz hammer. Hold the punch in one hand against the surface of the block and gently tap the punch so indenting the lead. At the same time move the punch gradually so that each successive blow over-laps the other and a smooth contour is achieved. This first inden-tation should be shallower than the final form required for it is advisable to form the sheet metal progressively in stages. Having produced a suitable indentation in the lead block place the sheet metal over the indentation and with the largest doming punch possible, force the metal into the indentation gradually, moving the punch so that successive blows overlap. At the end it may be necessary to use a slightly smaller diameter doming punch to impress the sheet properly into the lead. The formed metal is then removed from the block and the surfaces that have been in contact with the lead carefully buffed with emery or sandpaper to rid them of any trace of lead. The metal is then annealed. Any lead left on the work will burn in during the annealing process and spoil the job. Final forming is carried out by increasing the depth of the indentation with a slightly smaller punch and then using it to force the metal into the form required. It may be necessary to repeat this process several times before the desired contour is achieved. Finally, holding the stem of the punch in the vice and the metal form firmly on the punch, the outer surface is gently planished with a hammer against the punch to a smooth contour (Illus 57).

Doming

Metal can be domed in a simple device appropriately named a doming block. By using a variety of punches, domes of many dif-ferent diameters can be formed. The doming block in Illus 56 has a range of indentations which are suitably graduated and for which there are matching punches. Again it is essential that these tools are kept in good condition as any fault in punches or doming block is forced into the surface of the metal being manipulated, making more work at the finishing stage. The best way to polish punches is on the electric lathe.

Place a disc of metal in the largest indentation in the doming block and using the largest punch, which ought to have a slightly smaller diameter than that of the indentation (if you do not have a punch of the correct diameter, then the ball end of the ball pene hammer is a good substitute). Hold the punch firmly against the piece of metal in the block and tap with the 4oz hammer, not too fiercely otherwise you will stretch and thin the metal. Doming is a gradual process which should be carried out with care. Move the metal around in the block as you tap the punch so that it planishes every part of the disc evenly to make it form the exact shape of the indentation in the doming block.

The depth of the dome you put on the disc of metal is limited by its diameter relative to the diameter of the indentations in the

Illus 54

Illus 55

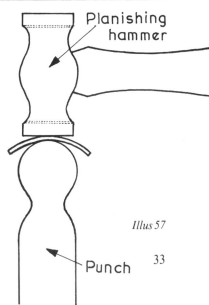

Planishing hammer

Illus 57

Illus 56

Punch

33

block. Always start at the larger indentations and move the metal you are working on to the smaller diameter till you reach the dome you require, all the time remembering to anneal the metal frequently during the operation. Further doming can be carried out by gripping a doming punch by the shank in the vice, having selected one which has a smaller diameter than that of the dome you have created in the block. Place the domed metal over the punch, hold it firmly against the punch and systematically tap with the flat of your hammer, preferably a small planishing hammer (Illus 57).

Raising Sheet Metal

Although the subject of raising and forging of sheet metal is exploited to a greater extent by silversmiths, the jeweller uses the same techniques, but of course on a smaller scale. So far the simple steel block and doming punch are the only form of stake considered, although the variety of stakes available are infinite and very many forms can be obtained, modifying the standard shapes by filing and grinding to suit particular applications.

To make the simple beaker shape in Illus 58 start with a circular blank of a suitable size (see p 159) and using a dome-ended mallet force it into a shallow dish shape made in the sandbag. It is usual to clamp the stake in a vice bolted to a stout bench and to sit on the bench during the operation (although some people prefer to stand in front of the vice and work). Gradually work with the mallet from the centre of the blank outwards in a spiral, ensuring that the whole surface has a smooth contour. Then using a pair of compasses pivoting on the centre of the blank, mark out pencil circles approximately 9mm apart beginning at the point where the raising should start to the outer edge. Select a suitably shaped stake on which to work and begin with the cross pene raising hammer, following the pencil lines. Work in a spiral out to the edge of the

Illus 58

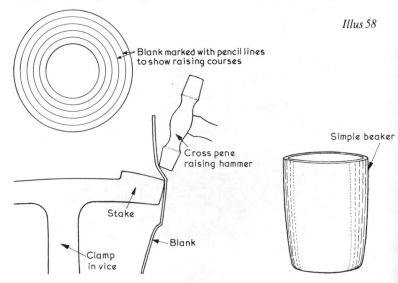

Blank marked with pencil lines to show raising courses

Cross pene raising hammer

Simple beaker

Stake

Clamp in vice

Blank

blank each blow overlapping the other. The effect is to bend the metal over the stake little by little until gradually the required form is achieved. At no time should the metal be stretched or impinged between stake and hammer. Ideally the thickness of the formed metal should be very nearly the same as that of the original blank. The number of times the metal has to be raised will depend on the complexity of the object being made, but for the raising shown about twelve complete courses will be required.

After each complete course of raising the metal should be annealed, and after each of the final three or four courses a process called corking may be carried out to actually increase the thickness of the top edge of the raised piece. The procedure is to hold the metal in a sandbag and beat down evenly all the way round the top edge with the raising hammer to force the metal back on itself and so thicken the edge (Illus 59).

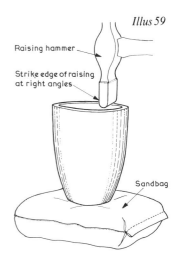

Illus 59

Raising hammer

Strike edge of raising at right angles

Sandbag

Templates

To assist in producing the required shape it is advisable to make a template of thick card, or preferably thin metal, which represents half of the sectional contour of the object. During the raising process this is held against the object to check that all is going well (Illus 60).

Planishing

To bring the raised surface to an even polished contour a *planishing hammer* with a highly polished face is used to strike the metal at the exact point where it is supported by the stake (Illus 61). It is essential that the hammer strikes the metal over the stake, and to ensure exactly where the point of contact is it is necessary to sound the surface by gently tapping with the hammer. Stakes should be selected that fit the contours of the object being worked on, and in

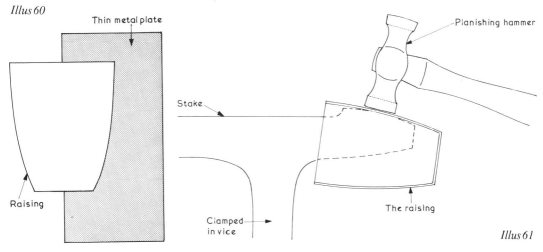

Illus 60

Thin metal plate

Stake

Raising

Clamped in vice

Planishing hammer

The raising

Illus 61

35

the case of a complex shape with several different curvatures it will be necessary to use several stakes for each part. It is important that the hammer strikes the metal absolutely squarely for any mark left by the edge of the hammer will be very difficult to remove. A spiralling movement is used beginning at the centre and moving outwards with each hammer blow overlapping. The effect is to produce a surface covered with tiny facets, the finish of which is imparted by the polished hammer face.

Chasing and Repoussé

Chasing, repoussé, or embossing, are carried out in a pitch filled cast iron hemispherical bowl which stands on a thick leather ring (Illus 62). The pitch is made to a special formula: 7lbs best Swedish brown pitch approx walnut size piece of 1) tallow 2) resin 3) best pumice powder or plaster of Paris, or sieved brick dust. Be careful not to put in too much of the last ingredients for more can always be added. Heat the pitch carefully in a thick pot with rounded bottom corners, add the other ingredients and stir well. To test the consistency of pitch when the mixture is thoroughly combined, pour a little on a cold slab. The quality can be judged by 'pulling out' the pitch – it should stretch to quite a long thread. The second test is the 'fingernail' test which is carried out when the pitch is at normal room temperature. It should only just take an impression of the fingernail. If pieces of broken brick are put in the bowl before filling it with pitch it will save a great deal. The bowl should be filled to the brim and the pitch allowed to cool and solidify. The object to be worked is then fastened in place by gently warming the pitch with a gas torch. Be careful not to burn it as it will deteriorate and be spoilt. (It may be necessary to build the pitch up into a mound to give the required working height by melting a little extra on to the surface of the filled bowl).

Repoussé

Repoussé is a term given to the process where metal is punched and hammered into relief from the reverse side and detailed with punches from the front. Embossing and repoussé is done with contoured hardened steel punches, some of which may be bought, but the majority, in particular the special shaped ones, have to be made (see page 13). A special hammer is required (Illus 63), which has an extra large flat striking face, a ball pene, and a specially designed slim handle with a spherical end for holding in the palm of the hand. It is usual to start work on the back of the object bumping areas into relief with doming punches. It is important to make the guide lines necessary for your work with a pencil, but remember that you are working in reverse. The punch is held against the first three fingers by the thumb, the little finger rests on the object or the pitch to act as a steady, the punch is held just off the surface of the metal and hit with the hammer. The drop hammer effect assists the process. For long runs with the

doming punch move it as you strike it so that each consecutive blow overlaps the other to give a smooth contour. Having raised the required areas remove the metal from the pitch by gentle warming, anneal it, and pickle in acid to clean. The object is then placed back in the pitch but this time with the front uppermost. Care should be taken that all the raised areas are filled from behind with pitch and it may be necessary to fill them prior to fastening in the pitch bowl. Having ensured all is correct work may be carried out with the small punches to bring out details of the relief.

Chasing

Chasing is a process of indentation and is carried out with highly finished gently contoured chisels. The metal is fixed into the pitch as before. The chisel is held in direct contact with the metal, at an angle away from you so that as the hammer blows hit it it works towards you, the trailing edge doing most of the work, the leading edge only just marking the metal (Illus 64, 65). Although hammering is an automatic technique it is necessary to concentrate. For straight lines and gentle curves a straight punch is used, while for curved lines and circles curved and ring punches are used. These punches can have patterns and textures cut in them in which case they are called *matting punches*. Sometimes when heavy work is done it may be necessary to file and Water of Ayre stone the metal which is thrown up on either side of the indentation. A small sharpened chisel can be used to actually cut metal away, a technique the Indian jewellers use to great effect to give bright highlights to their 22ct gold work.

Illus 64

Illus 65

Punch works towards operator

Chasing punch

Trailing corner of punch

Metal shape set in pitch bowl

3 Soldering and Annealing

Equipment

For both these processes you will need a certain amount of equipment. A hearth on which to work can be made by covering a surface with asbestos sheet. Its size will depend on the type of work you are doing. A hearth of the dimensions of the one in Illus 66a is suitable for large items such as the silversmith deals with and is very useful if you have the space and money. But if you are mainly concerned with smaller jewellery work it is a luxury. A simpler, cheaper arrangement is an asbestos pad and a fire brick with a sheet of gauze on top as in Illus 66b. In fact this is all I use. The fire

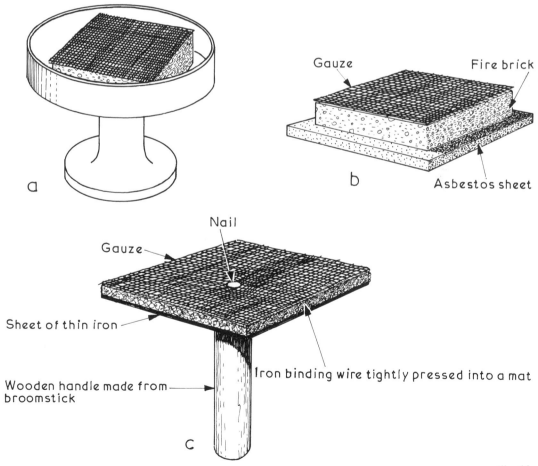

Illus 66

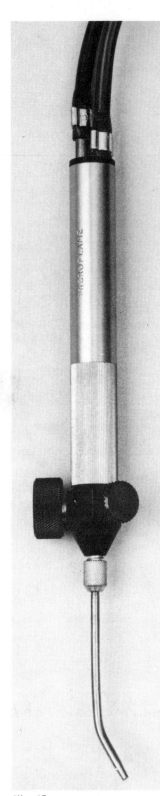

Illus 67

brick can come from an old fireplace, but the asbestos available from jewellers' suppliers must be of the correct type suitable for the direct contact with the flame. Never use builders' roofing asbestos cement sheeting, as it explodes when heated. The hand held soldering boss (Illus 66c) is also useful.

There are many types of gas torches for heating, and the type chosen will depend on the gas supply available. There are a variety of coal gas and traditional soldering torches which are very versatile and well tried. Natural gas is not as versatile as coal gas and although there are torches available the ranges of flame size are limited. One satisfactory method where a mains gas supply is not available is to use bottle propane or butane gas cylinders with an appropriate gas torch available from the gas suppliers. Although expensive, the combination of oxygen and propane through regulator valves to a small hand torch similar to a welding torch is very satisfactory. Examples suitable for either oxy-propane or oxy-acetylene are shown in Illus 67, 68. Personally I prefer the former which is not so hot and a lot cleaner. With either arrangement, the size of work that can be done with them is limited, but for the purposes of most jewellers they are very good.

The traditional jewellers' French blow torch, featured in Illus 69 is the simplest and cheapest soldering torch. It works off coal gas and has a simple hand tap which gives a pilot light when in the out-of-use position, and when turned gives an accurate flame control up to full gas pressure. Air is introduced to the flame with the aid of a mouth blow pipe held in the mouth. This system is traditionally very suitable for intricate work and although takes some time to master is very versatile. A variation of this torch can be connected to a compressed air supply to replace the mouth-held tube.

For large work on the big hearth a torch supplemented by either a bellows or compressor to feed a sufficient quantity of air to it can be used. But compressors are a luxury in a small workshop and there are a number of bottled gas torches suitable for this work which do not need compressed air.

One way of soldering is with an electric resistance soldering machine. The job is clipped to one electrode and the circuit completed by a carbon point applied to the solder before the current is switched on. Temperature is controlled by adjusting the amount of current put out by the unit which can produce enough heat to melt platinum, or at the other end of the scale just enough heat to melt lead solder. Although giving a very useful localised heat, this system needs a lot of practice to work properly for it is very difficult to see when the solder has melted and if the current is too high it will melt your work. It is useful for localised heating and melting to produce texture.

A useful implement that can be easily made is a soldering or annealing boss. This is constructed as in Illus 66c and is very useful for heating large items, particularly flat sheets of metal. The gauze top surface allows the heat to pass under and over the

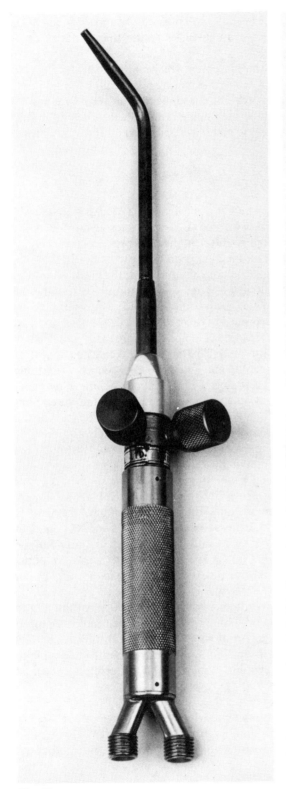

Illus 68

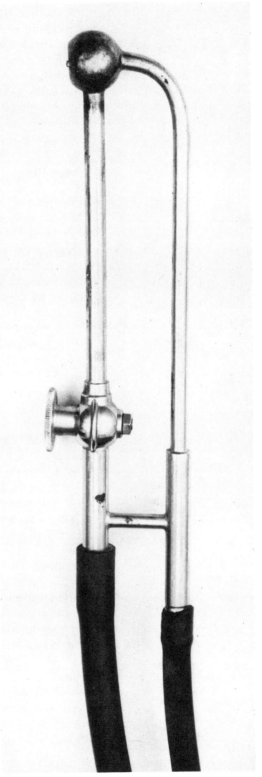

Illus 69

object, the minimal contact between the object and the surface of the boss reduces the heat loss by conductivity and the metal heats easily and evenly. It is much easier to use than a flat piece of asbestos for example.

Having selected the equipment you require the next thing is to learn how to use it. For either soldering or annealing it is advisable to work in a shaded area. Strong sunlight or artificial light are not to be recommended as they make it difficult to observe the condition and colour of the metal as it is heated and you may melt it by mistake.

Annealing

It is essential to learn how to anneal metal, a process which has to be done when metal is worked to remove stresses introduced by rolling out, hammering, and bending, and prevent it cracking or breaking up. The metal is placed on the hearth and with a large open flame the temperature is raised to bring the metal to an even dull cherry red. It is then allowed to cool gradually. Judging the exact point when metal needs annealing can only come with experience, but if it feels hard to work then it needs annealing. Most items, especially those in sheet metal, are more easily annealed on the gauze surface. But more care has to be taken when annealing wire. Thick diameters (0.9mm +) can be easily coped with. Long lengths are wound accurately into coils about 120mm in diameter and tied with binding wire at about six points around the circumference as in Illus 70. A large open flame is used as for sheet metal. If a concentrated sharp localised flame is used uneven annealing will occur, certain areas overheat and become brittle and liable to break when manipulated. Move the flame continuously round the coil never allowing it to linger on any one spot until a dull cherry red colour is achieved throughout the coil. When annealing fine wire from a hair's thickness to 0.7mm, the wire is wrapped round a tin, such as a bean tin with the ends cut out. Cut a notch in one end of the tin with shears into which the end of the wire can be attached. Coil the wire tightly round the exterior of the tin and then attach the loose ends to a notch cut in the other end of the tin, making sure that the wire is tight to the tin and not raised from it at any point. Place the tin on the gauze and direct the flame, which should not be too fierce, in the open end of the tin so heating the whole length of wire which is evenly annealed when the tin is a dull red heat. Very fine wire is virtually impossible to anneal using an open flame, making the tin technique essential (Illus 71).

After annealing the metal must be cleaned of oxide by acid. I have found that battery acid, which is one part sulphuric acid to three parts water, is suitable. It is available at many garages and chemists. To make this solution from concentrated sulphuric acid *always add acid to water never water to acid, as the reaction is so violent that it is very dangerous.* The acid should be kept warm in a

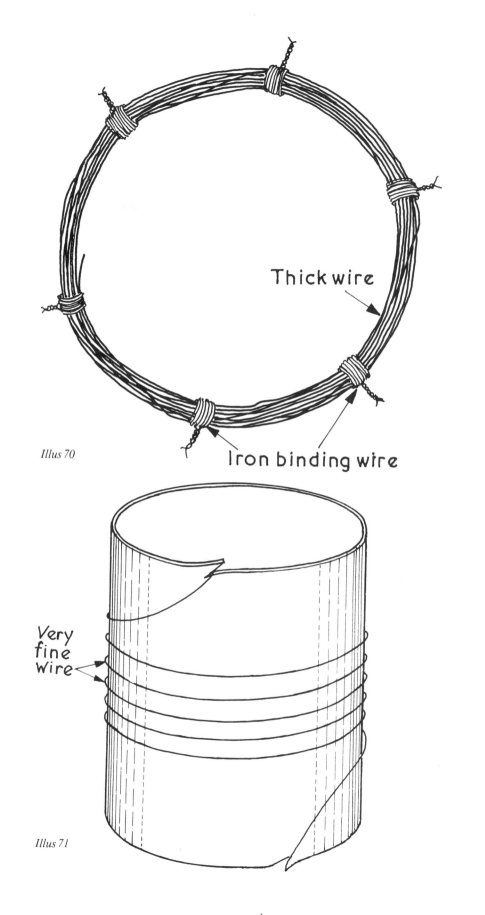

Thick wire

Iron binding wire

Illus 70

Very fine wire

Illus 71

43

lead or Pyrex container on a low gas jet or on an electric ring. Do not boil. The metal should be tied to a copper wire or held in copper tongs and dipped in the warm acid and then rinsed thoroughly in water. Never put iron or steel into the acid as this will instantly contaminate and ruin the acid. If acid gets onto clothing, skin or eyes, wash thoroughly. On clothing a solution of sodium bicarbonate and water will neutralise the acid. Non-acid pickle which is not so harmful to skin or clothing and requires less ventilation is bought in granular form, dissolved in water as recommended, and used hot. When available this solution is strongly recommended on the grounds of safety.

Soldering

Good soldering is a matter of practice. You will make many mistakes but you will learn a great deal from them. Silver, gold and platinum solderings are simple processes as long as the basic rules are remembered:
1   Cleanliness
2   Correct fluxing
3   Do not try to fill gaps with solder
4   Correct quantity of soldering alloy
5   Do not overheat

Solders come in many alloy forms and have a wide range of melting points, silver solder being available with about six different melting points. The reason for this is that in a complicated job with many solderings (Illus 104 Ch 4) the initial work can be done with the high melting point (HMP) solders and subsequent solderings carried out with the lower melting point (LMP) ones. However, in the beginning use one of the medium melting ones (MMP) as they flow more easily than HMP solders which are a little more tricky to work with. Gold solders are available to suit the particular gold alloy being used whether it is white or yellow gold. Gold soldering is very simple, but the difference between the melting point of the gold and its solder is less than between copper and silver solder, therefore the risk of melting is greater, especially with the HMP solder. 22ct gold has only one grade of solder, which will flow just before the gold itself melts, as does hard 18ct solder. Although the medium and easy solders are much more manageable, the beauty of gold, particularly 18ct alloys, is that polished surfaces can be protected from the effects of heating and soldering by the use of boric acid powder mixed with methylated spirit in the proportion of 1:2. The polished gold is simply dipped in this solution, so leaving a fine layer of boric acid on the surface. On heating this melts and forms a very effective protective flux against oxidation which can be easily removed after soldering in hot acid pickle or boiling water. Boric acid, whilst very effective on gold, is not nearly so effective on other metals such as silver and copper, although it is sometimes useful.

Soldering alloys are generally bought in sheets and accurate and economical cutting is essential. Cut into the solder with the shears in one direction and then cut across these cuts so making small square panels which can be caught on the finger against the lower blade of the shears (Illus 72, 73). Great accuracy and continuity in size can be achieved by this method. The sizes of panels can be altered by varying the distance between cuts. Nothing is more wasteful than solder which has been hacked about with the shears. It also means that quantities of solder cannot be properly assessed if panels of irregular shape are cut. Solder can also be bought prepared as filings which are applied to the spot with a fluxing brush. They are very useful for some hollow work and if you have a lot of links to solder together.

Prepare the surface for soldering making sure that it is free from dirt and grease. This is done with files or emery paper before washing in hot water and detergent. Both panels and the metal to be soldered must be evenly covered with a flux. There are two types in common use, the traditional one being borax which is very suitable for silver, gilding metal, copper and brass. The second, bought in solution form, is more suitable for platinum and gold. But borax is probably the best all round flux for the beginner. It comes in the form of a solid white cone with a slate (Illus 74). It is ground on the slate with a small quantity of water to produce a

Illus 73

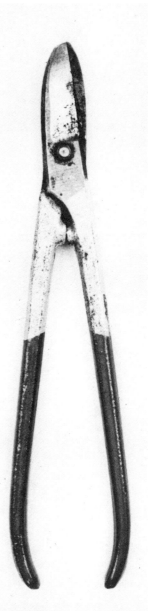

Illus 72

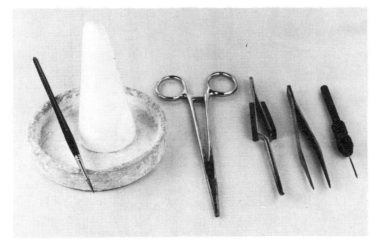

Illus 74 Left to right: borax cone plate and brush; arterial forceps; sprung corn tongs; corn tongs; steel needle in pin vice

45

milky solution. This should be quite fluid and of an even colour. A pasty solution means excessive borax on the soldering area which on heating will cause a great deal of bubbling, with solder panels flying everywhere, the metal moving about, and general chaos. A thin, even layer of flux is applied with a small cheap paint brush. Then, using the wet fluxing brush place the solder panels in the appropriate positions. It is important to apply enough solder to slightly overfill the joint, as insufficient solder makes a weak link. However, too much is ugly and the excess often very difficult to remove.

At first the metal is gently warmed to slowly evaporate the water. Too much heat at this stage will cause boiling and the solder will flick all over the place. Use a steel pointer such as a needle held in a pin vice to control the position of the solder. Once the water has evaporated more heat can be applied as the flux melts and glues the solder in position. You should then begin to see the solder melt. Keep the heat going until the solder flows – it is important that you can see it flowing properly. Sometimes a beginner stops heating after the solder has melted but before it has flowed for fear of melting the metal. This makes a sort of tack soldering which is very weak and totally unsatisfactory. A beginner is generally soldering copper or gilding metal – both very difficult to overheat. If however the solder is overheated, it will eat into the surface of the metal, making a crater.

There are many jigs available for soldering operations and these can be used to advantage when binding wire and tongs won't solve the problems of holding one part accurately against another

Illus 75

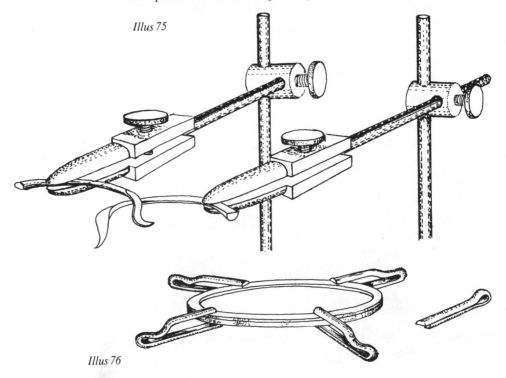

Illus 76

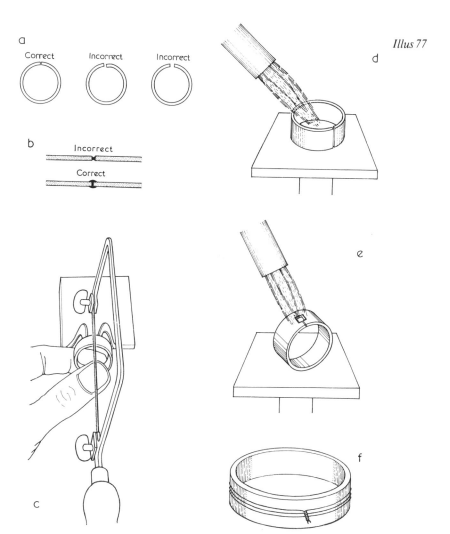

whilst being soldered (Illus 75). Cotter pins (split pins) as used by engineers may be used to clip one piece of metal to another during soldering (Illus 76).

Simple soldering, such as in making a ring or setting can be done by bending the strip of metal around with a pair of half round and flat parallel nosed pliers (Illus 77a). It is important that the two ends are filed square so that they do this accurately, as soldering relies on the capillary action caused by the close proximity of two surfaces (Illus 77b). If after shaping the ends do not close properly, then simply pass a saw blade between them. This will accurately true the faces off to conform with each other as in Illus 77c, the gap can be closed by further bending. Flux the joint, anneal the ring to remove stresses, check that the joint is tightly closed and solder (Illus 77d, 77e).

When soldering rings or bands some people bind the band around the diameter with iron wire. This does help but with smaller diameters is unnecessary if the annealing has been done properly. When soldering bands of over 100mm in diameter, it is necessary to tie binding wire round to assist in keeping the two edges together when distortion occurs (Illus 77f). Binding wire is invaluable in constructional work. One of the best ways to keep and use the coil is to cut it in half, store one half, bind the other with wire to keep the coils together. This second coil is cut right through with shears at one point, so that as you require a length you can just pull a piece out without turning the coil into a tangled mass (Illus 78). The stored half can be used when longer lengths of wire are required which can be cut accordingly.

Illus 78

4 Intricate Work

Simple and effective jewellery can be easily and quickly made with wire. It can be turned into squares, rings, or ovals which can be combined in flat or three-dimensional shapes to create an infinite variety of objects from chains to applied decoration. It is important not to underestimate the full potential of this simple form of metal which has been used extensively by jewellers throughout the centuries.

Before beginning work instead of using the conventional pencil design to follow, try pieces of string glued to card and made into models. This gives a greater idea of thickness and is very effective.

Wire can be reduced in diameter and for this steel draw plates or dies are required. A draw plate has a sequence of graduated holes through which the wire is drawn and these are available in a variety of hole shapes: half round, round, square, triangular, knife edge, double half round, and rectangular. Before the wire is drawn it has to be very carefully tapered as it is essential that it is fed into the plate gradually and smoothly. To do this file a groove in a flat piece of wood or bench peg and, holding the wire firmly in a pin vice place it in the groove and file it with a broad flat file on all sides (Illus 79) until a gentle taper is achieved. Round wire is rotated in the groove and at the same time filed to taper evenly. Before drawing, rub beeswax or put oil on the wire, grip the draw plate in a vice and pass the tapered point through the required hole. With a stout pair of pliers draw the wire firmly and steadily through the hole. Any jerking will stretch or even break the wire

Illus 79

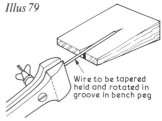

Wire to be tapered held and rotated in groove in bench peg

Illus 80

or give uneven dimensions down the length (Illus 80).

The draw bench is a more sophisticated device and consists of a simple arrangement for holding the draw plate and a pair of jaws which clamp onto the wire pulling it through by means of a hand winch. But even with this tool care and smooth operation is essential for good results. Frequent annealing is necessary, usually after every third reduction, and it is essential that the annealing is even, otherwise hard spots which can cause breakage or stretching, will result.

To form simple links or rings the wire is turned round a mandrel of suitable dimensions and shape. Mandrels should preferably be made of ferrous material. Round loops are turned round a circular mandrel which together with one end of the wire is clamped in a hand vice. The mandrel is then supported against the bench peg and turned. It is important that the wire is pulled taut as it is turned on to the mandrel (Illus 81). To make oval, square and other shaped links which require mandrel shapes other than round the mandrel has to be tightly bound with a strip of thin brown wrapping paper about 25mm wide (Illus 82). When the coiling has been completed the whole lot including the mandrel and paper are brought up to annealing temperature causing the paper to burn away, and leaving the coiled wire free to slide off the mandrel. If this is not done it will be virtually impossible to remove the coil. Slide the coil down to the end of the mandrel and, supporting it against the bench peg, saw the rings off using either a piercing saw or a back saw (Illus 83). These can be used to form a simple chain constructed by closing a few rings together and soldering them with tiny panels of solder. They can then be hooked together with open links which can in turn be soldered (Illus 84). The variations of design are infinite using different shaped links.

A simple technique for producing irregular shaped links or repeatable shapes in wire is by making a form around which the wire can be shaped (Illus 85). Small nails can be driven into a reasonably thick piece of wood which is able to stand rigid. The

Illus 81

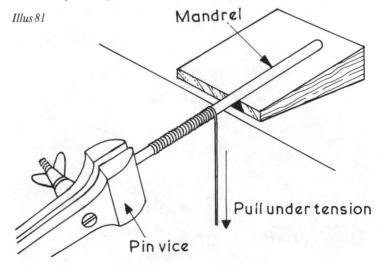

Mandrel

Pull under tension

Pin vice

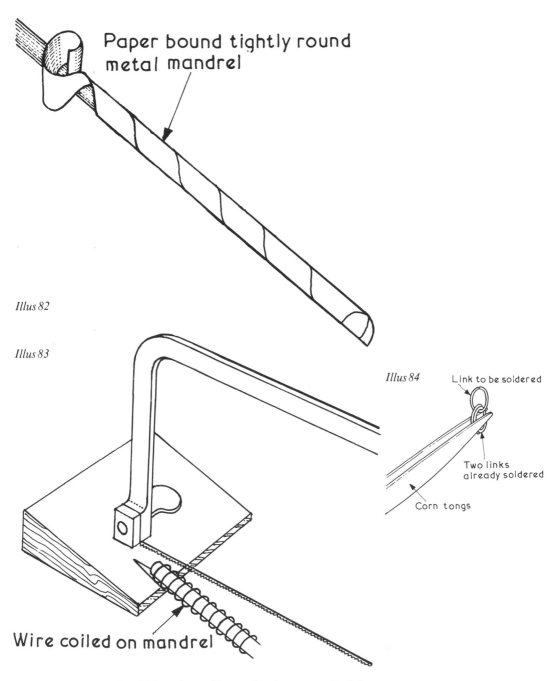

Paper bound tightly round metal mandrel

Illus 82

Illus 83

Illus 84

Link to be soldered

Two links already soldered

Corn tongs

Wire coiled on mandrel

heads of the nails should be taken off to make the removal of the wire easier. The wire is wound around the nails and in this way the same shape can be repeated several times.

Twisted Wire

Wire can be twisted into rope-like lengths with a makeshift hook and a vice. The wire has first to be evenly annealed, then it is doubled and the two ends clamped in a bench vice. The hook can

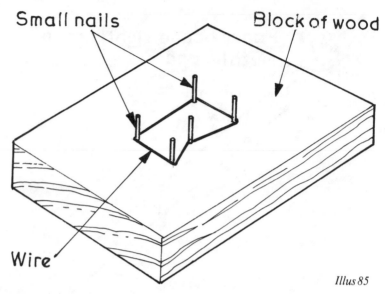

Small nails **Block of wood**

Wire

be held in the hand drill or hand vice. Hook the loop of wire to be twisted, pull taut and start turning, making sure that the wire is always under tension, otherwise kinking and buckling will occur. This technique has been exploited to a great extent for filigree work, where twists of various sizes are combined in a design. Differing sections or several strands of wire may be twisted together. Some of the strands can then be carefully peeled out to give a totally different effect. This type of work can be applied to sheet metal as decoration or soldered together to form open work. Great care should be taken, because you will be soldering small pieces to larger pieces.

Cork Screw

A traditional technique used to surround cameos is to combine wire with thin metal strips to form a decorative cork screw effect. It is constructed by taking a strip of metal about 3mm wide by 0.25mm thick and two lengths of wire approx 0.9mm in diameter. The ends of all three are clamped in the bench vice after they have been annealed, with the strip between the wires which must be carefully positioned down the centre of the strip (Illus 86). The other ends are held in a hand vice or with broad nose flat pliers again with the wires down the centre of the metal. All three are pulled under equal tension so as to actually stretch the metal,

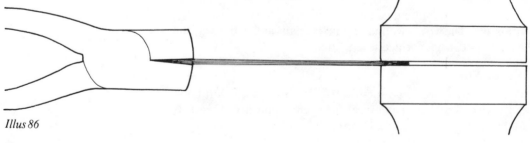

causing them to come together with no spaces between. They are then twisted until the wire closes tightly on to the strip. At no time must the wires be released otherwise you will be in difficulties. The wire can then be removed carefully, leaving the strip in its cork screw form. A similar effect can be achieved by twisting the strip only, but this tends not to be uniform, and because it cannot be twisted to a sufficient extent without the metal collapsing, the effect is not a true cork screw.

Drilling

Drilling holes in metal is an important technique for the jeweller who may use it to form linking mechanisms, suitable holes to set stones in or simple decoration may be contrived using a variety of drill sizes to give a range of hole sizes arranged to make a pattern.

There are many types of drill stock available, from simple Archemedian types to sophisticated powered models. The tra-

Illus 87

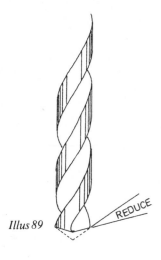

Illus 89

REDUCE

ditional jeweller's drill stock (Illus 90) is an inexpensive device which has proved to be very versatile and most suitable for fine work, for when handled properly a great deal of control can be exercised.

Before drilling it is essential to mark the surface of the metal with a small indentation exactly at the point where the hole is to go. This is done with a centre punch or spit-stick depending on which is most suitable for the job in hand. A spit-stick is used for delicate work (details on page 68). The sharp point is pressed into the metal and revolved, making the necessary mark ready for the drill (Illus 87). If you are using a centre punch which requires a hammer blow, the metal directly below the point of the punch must be supported firmly from behind on a steel block (Illus 88). Some centre punches have a spring loaded device in the handle. This mechanism is compressed by hand pressure on the handle of the punch causing the spring to release and make an impact inside the punch producing the necessary force to cause the indentation by the point. Although it has a device for controlling the impact

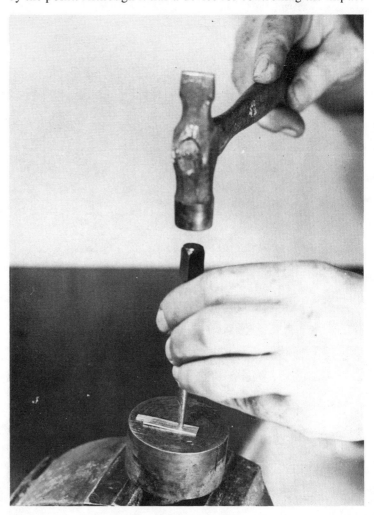

Illus 88

adequate support of the metal is essential.

To pierce the metal always start by using a drill much smaller in diameter than the hole required and enlarge the opening as necessary with a bigger drill. If the diameters are too similar the drill will jam causing an irregular shape. This technique gives the opportunity of correction and also makes for greater accuracy. When using small diameter drills run them at high speeds under light pressure with a small spot of light sewing machine oil or spittle for lubrication. To pierce thin sheet metal when the point of the drill pierces the sheet before the shoulder of the drill enters the metal, it is necessary to reduce the angle of the cutting faces so that the drill does not cut so deeply but merely scrapes its way through the sheet metal (Illus 89). Sometimes it is advisable to turn the sheet and finish off the drilling from the other side.

The jeweller's bow type drill stock is supplied with a variety of chuck sizes to suit different drills. With this type of stock it is essential that the small diameter (1mm and less) drill bits are gripped in the chuck with a small length of drill protruding. The

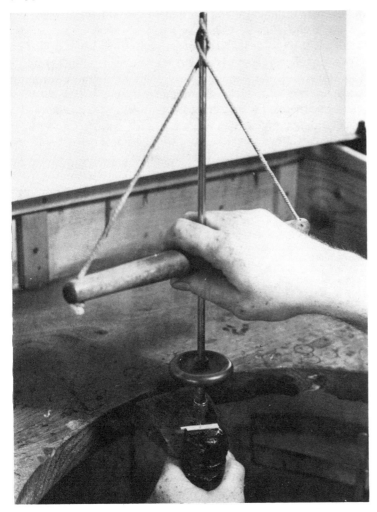

Illus 90

weight of the bow drill is such that if the length of the drill bit is too excessive it will wobble and probably break. To work this drill, place your hand on the wooden cross piece with the vertical steel rod coming between your centre fingers, the wooden rod lying in line with the middle knuckles of the fingers (Illus 90). Check that the wooden spar is at right angles with the vertical steel spindle and then turn the fly wheel in an anti-clockwise direction so that the thong winds itself around the centre spindle. Place the drill point where the hole has to be pierced and apply light pressure to the wooden spar of the drill stock. The thong will untwist so revolving the drill but the art is to release downward pressure on the spar when the thong has unwound so allowing momentum to rewind it around the vertical spindle so that the cycle may be repeated over and over, keeping the drill continually revolving. With practice skill will develop, making the instrument very suitable for stone fitting and other operations where control is important.

Besides the various sizes of twist drill a useful tool to have is a spade ended drill, which you can make yourself from an ordinary sewing needle (Illus 91). The advantage of this is that it can be fitted into the bow drill and is not so fragile as the twist drill. The conventional geared hand drill stock available from many hardware stores is also very useful for drills larger than those normally used in the bow drill stock. But it requires the use of both hands to operate it whereas the bow drill can be worked with one hand, the other holding the metal steady.

If you can afford a pendant drill with a flexible drive it is a very useful piece of equipment. They are supplied with a variety of chuck sizes and a vast range of attachments are available from simple twist drills, through all the dental drill range of burrs to emery impregnated rubber shapes for removing scratches and tiny felt, calico, and bristle polishing spindles (see page 26).

Vertical drilling machines are a luxury in a small workshop but

Illus 91 a break the needle at g; b grind the surface flat on an oil stone; c grind the sides flat; d, e, f grind the two cutting faces

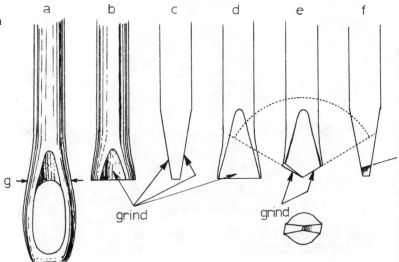

they are very useful. If you are buying one it is advisable to choose a machine with a variety of speeds, so that the machine can be adjusted to suit drill sizes and the material being drilled.

Making Fittings

Most of the fittings you will need are shown in Illus 92–97 and are more or less self-explanatory needing only simple soldering techniques. But there are certain details relating to their location on a piece of jewellery which a craftsman needs to know.

Brooch Pins

Brooch fittings have to be positioned in a certain way if they are to work properly. The line along which the joint and catch are placed has to be above the centre line of the brooch, in other words the brooch is suspended by the pin with most of its weight below. If the heavier part of the brooch is above the pin it will fall forwards and never lie properly. The joint and catch when looking at the back of the brooch should lie with the joint to the right with its closed side facing inwards. The catch should lie to the left with the opening for the pin facing downwards (Illus 94B). The pin should be kept as springy as possible and should lever on the joint so that it has to be sprung into the catch (Illus 94A). The length of the pin is important for an excessively long pin can be dangerous and a short one will not function correctly.

In a wire hook type catch as in Illus 93(2), the point of the pin should protrude by about 2mm. For the safety catch similar to

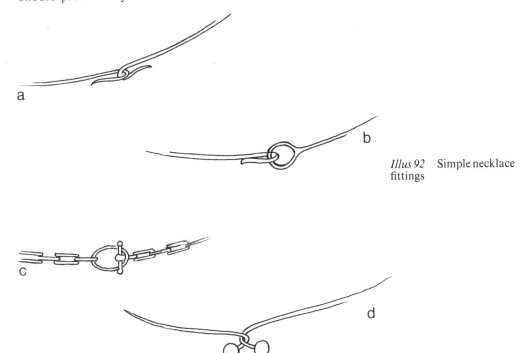

Illus 92   Simple necklace fittings

1	13 4	0·5-0·6	Fold metal and drill	Piece from centre File to shape	(image)	BOOK JOINT FOR BROOCH
2	Round wire 12	0·9-1·0 File gentle angled flat at one end	Bend to form catch	File flat for soldering to brooch		HOOK CATCH FOR BROOCH
3	Round wire long enough to form loop and pass thro brooch catch. Wire must be drawn hard.	0·9-1·0	Turn ring on end of wire and solder	To re-harden twist wire holding loop half turn one way back to normal. Half turn other way back to normal	Incorrect weak pin Correct strong pin	BROOCH PIN
4	3 5 12 6	0·8 0·6				SAFETY BROOCH CATCH
5	3 3 32 18	1·0 3·0	13 4 15			CUFF LINK FITTING
6	2 5 50	0·6 0·8				SAFETY EAR FITTINGS
7		0·5 0·8 0·5				FRENCH WIRES
8	2 5 dia 2 dia 40 12	0·8 0·5 0·6 Inside dia	Cut thread in tube Cut thread on wire			SCREW FITTINGS

Illus 93

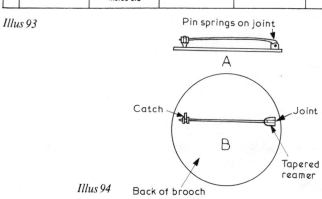

Pin springs on joint

A

Catch — Joint

B

Tapered reamer

Illus 94   Back of brooch

that in Illus 93(4), the pin should not protrude at all but be exactly flush with the outside edge of the catch.

The fitting of the pin into the joint is important and it must be accurately carried out. The pin should slip into the joint and the holes line up. If this does not happen then careful filing should be carried out with a smooth file until the pin is adjusted into place. Once a good fit has been achieved it is necessary to line the holes up and pass a tapered steel broach (Illus 95) through them to align and open them out to take the tapered rivet on which the pin pivots. There is a particular direction in which the tapered reamer must be inserted. It is held in a pin vice and inserted from the bottom of the brooch upwards. It is never inserted from the top downwards. The reason is that if at a later date the pin has to be removed, then the direction of removal of the rivet is not a problem.

To make a rivet that will pass through the joint a piece of wire of about the same diameter as that used for the pin should be used. This is held in a pin vice and accurately tapered with a smooth flat file. The taper should ideally be exactly the same as that of the broach. To do this file a shallow groove in the bench peg using the corner of a file and place the wire from which the rivet is being made in the groove. Start filing, at the same time rotating the pin vice so that the wire is filed equally all the way round. (This same technique is used to sharpen a point on the brooch pin, the shape of which is shown in Illus 93). The tapered wire is inserted through the joint and pin in the same direction as the broach. Holding the pin vice, force the tapered wire securely home with a twisting action. The brooch pin should not fall under its own weight but be a frictional fit on the rivet. The wire forming the rivet is trimmed off using either end or side cutting pliers, which leave just sufficient material for final riveting (Illus 96).

There are two methods of spreading the ends of the rivet. The simplest is by holding the larger end firmly against a steel block and with a small riveting hammer carefully tap the other end until it has expanded sufficiently to retain the rivet. Both ends of the rivet may be treated in this way and any roughness removed with a fine needle file. The other technique which is effective and quick requires a specially adapted pair of flat nosed pliers. A dimple is cut into each of the jaw faces with a 2mm drill (Illus 97). The dimples must be directly opposite each other and be close to the front edge of the pliers. The rivet is gripped in the pliers with the dimples located over the ends of the rivet and pressure applied. At the same time the pliers should be waggled backwards and forwards to burnish the ends of the rivets into polished beads.

Illus 95

Tubing

Tubing can be bought in a range of sizes or alternatively may be made. Its applications can be mechanical, hinges, settings, fittings etc or arranged to form decorative areas using different lengths and diameters to form patterns and contrasts (Illus 98).

Ready made tube has standardised wall thicknesses and so does

59

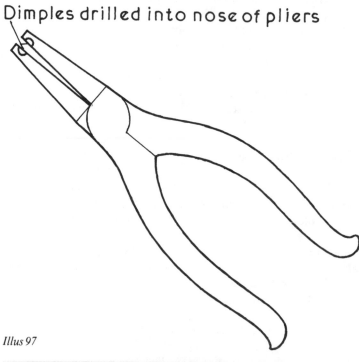

Dimples drilled into nose of pliers

Illus 97

Illus 96

Illus 98

not suit every application. It is therefore essential to be able to make tubing, particularly if working in copper and its alloys, which are not available in the small sizes required. Determine the wall thickness required of the tubing and select a suitable piece of sheet metal. From this cut a strip the width of which should be ap-

60

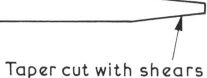

Taper cut with shears

proximately three times the diameter of the finished tube. With
the shears cut the end of this strip to a point (Illus 99). Then cut a
half-round groove in a piece of wood and, selecting a round metal
bar of a suitable radius, force the strip of metal into the groove
until it has been bent into a U-section. Pass the point of the strip
through a large hole in a draw plate, and with a pair of heavy wire
drawing tongs pull it through, while at the same time holding a
pair of flat nosed pliers across the tube at the back of the draw
plate so as to stop it from twisting (Illus 100). As the tube is moved
through successively smaller holes it is reduced, the flat nose pliers
gradually guiding the two edges until they come together and
butt accurately. Care should be taken that the edges do not overlap as this will spoil the tube, making it useless. The seam can then
be soldered and the tube is ready for use.

When constructing a hinge always ensure there is a substantial
foundation on which to solder the tubing (Illus 101) by in some

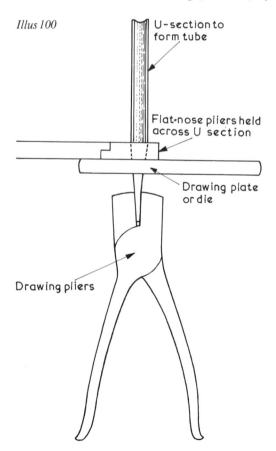

Illus 100

U-section to form tube

Flat-nose pliers held across U section

Drawing plate or die

Drawing pliers

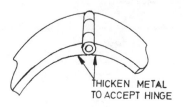

THICKEN METAL
TO ACCEPT HINGE

Illus 101

Illus 102   a and b width and thickness – the whole bangle is constructed of this. Band A is turned up, soldered and trued. Centre lines are scribed on it; c two ovals are cut from sheet; the centre lines of the oval are scribed on the metal. With an engraving tool (graver) raise a number of tiny spikes by cutting into the metal D. Part A can be located over these. The centre lines on A are located with those on B and they are bound with binding wire and soldered together. The centre is then cut out of B and the same procedure carried out with C. The centre is then cut out of C; d two strips of metal 0.55mm thick and wider than the bangle are cut to form the outer surface (E and F). E is soldered in place first, its ends lining up with the centre lines of the bangle on which the hinge and snap will later be positioned; e F is then soldered to fit neatly with the bangle sides and to butt against E. A tiny hole is drilled on the inside at G; f two diameters of the tube are used for the hinge. The larger is an exact fit over the inner. The larger is cut to a length slightly greater than the width of the bracelet. The small tube is cut into three; g the large tube is fitted and soldered into the bracelet. A segment is cut out H. The small tube sections are placed into the large tube with a piece of steel blued in a flame passing through them. They are carefully tacked as shown with tiny panels of solder; h the snap is constructed as shown. The tissue paper is used to stop solder running in between the two pieces of metal; i the snap is fitted by cutting a groove almost through the bangle and fitting part J and tacking it there with solder. The bangle is separated by cutting through at X and Y and filing the top off of J. All parts that were previously tacked are properly soldered. Part K is fitted and soldered in one side of the bangle. A rivet is fitted through the hinge and the bangle polished and finished. A back saw as in Illus 103 is best for cutting through at X and Y.

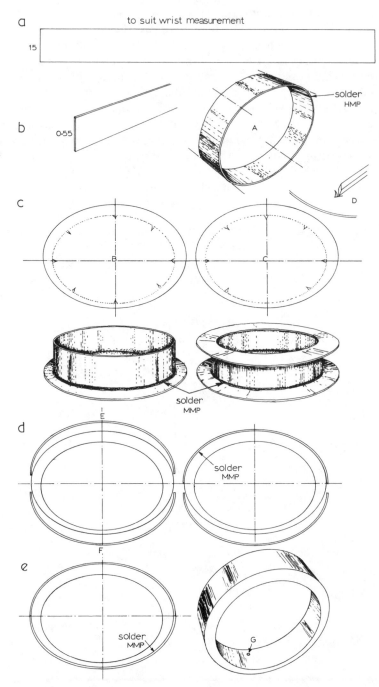

a   to suit wrist measurement

15

b   0·55

solder HMP

A

D

c   B   C

solder MMP

d   E   F   solder MMP

e   solder MMP   G

62

way thickening the metal where it is to be attached. File grooves in the edge of the metal so that the tubes can be accommodated. Put them in place with a steel rod through the centre to keep them in line. Place a small panel of solder on each tube in the appropriate place with the very minimum of flux and then heat until it just tacks each section of tube in position. The hinge is then separated and a little more solder applied to each of the tubes which are soldered finally in position.

Illus 102, 103 and 104 illustrate the steps in making an 18ct gold and diamond hollow bangle, designed and made by Kathleen McHugh.

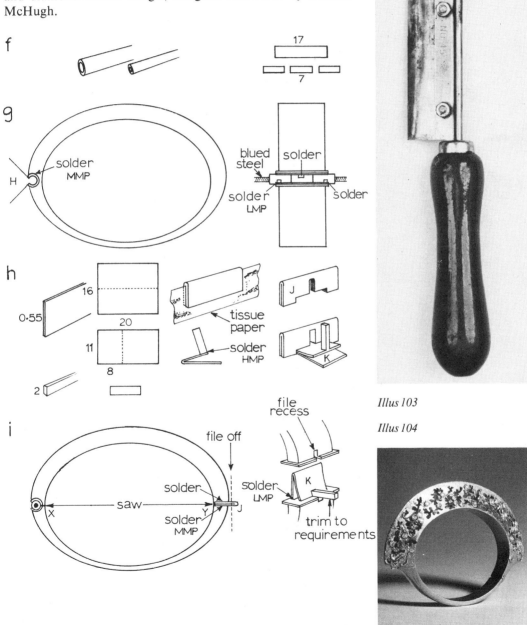

Illus 103

Illus 104

5 Stones and Their Settings

Metal shapes, although decorative in their own right, can be enhanced by stones; precious gems, elaborately cut, or simple agates found on the beaches and polished. Through the ages the methods of setting the stones have developed alongside the different techniques of cutting and shaping them. Each setting has to be made to fit its particular stone, and it is important that the type of setting is suitable to the cut of the stone.

Equipment

Apart from the usual range of equipment, certain extra implements shown in Illus 105 will be needed for setting the stone in place. Suitable handles are fitted on by clamping the tool in a vice with only the unhardened tang protruding. This relieves the hardened blade from any stress likely to shatter it. The handle is then simply hammered onto the tang but remember to check frequently to make sure that it goes on straight. The points of the scorpers are ground and sharpened to the correct angle (Illus 106).

A pusher (Illus 107) is a simple instrument for pressing metal over the girdle of the stone and it can easily be made from a piece of soft steel approximately 3.2mm in diameter – a nail with its head taken off will do – fitted into a scorper handle. If the pusher is too long or too short then control is affected. The way to judge the ideal length is to hold the pusher handle in the palm of your hand and see if your thumb can easily reach the end of the pusher. The end is filed square. The working surface should be gently roughened by tapping with a smooth flat file. It is essential that the surface is kept rough like this to prevent the tool slipping and possibly breaking a stone. A set of graining tools will be needed for pavé setting, or for setting stones into the surface of metal (Illus 107). These consist of handles with a number of interchangeable tapered metal rods, each with an indentation in the end. The indentations are graduated in size and it is necessary to select the right one – determined by the amount of metal to be grained.

It is of course very important in all setting operations that the metal is held securely. For rings you will require a pair of wooden clamps (Illus 108), for other items a shellac stick (Illus 105). The stick can be made from a piece of circular wood approximately 25–35mm in diameter and about 150mm long. (A piece of broom handle is suitable). On this build up a knob of shellac, which can be bought in the form of flakes and of fine lemon quality, by melt-

9ct yellow gold pendant set with heart-shaped amethysts, embossed to give the relief to the leaf-like structure; Designed and made by Susan Whitehead

64

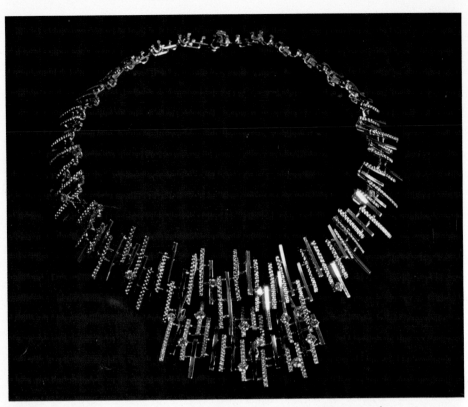

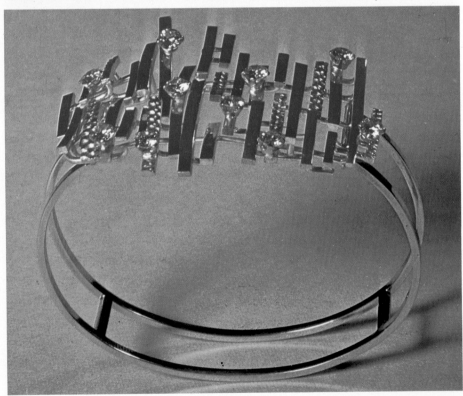

ing some of the flakes gently in a tin lid and dabbing the end of the stick in the molten mass covering the wood to about half an inch down its length. More shellac flakes can be applied to the initial layer and melted in a flame so that the knob is built up in layers. To shape the knob while in its molten state, hold it against a cold steel block, and by revolving and modelling, form a knob suitable for holding the work piece. Shellac does not stick to cold steel but it will grip warm material such as wood or skin. If you get hot shellac on your finger dip it in cold water and gently pull it off. If you try to tear it off while it is still hot you are liable to pull your skin away as well.

When needed for use the shellac is softened in a flame and the object to be supported sunk into it. To remove the article, chip the shellac away with a flat scorper or similar instrument. A small amount of heat can also be applied, but be careful of the stones as many of them are liable to suffer damage (see page 85). To dissolve all traces of shellac from the piece of jewellery soak it in methylated spirits, a process which can be hastened by boiling the spirits very carefully in the device shown in Illus 109. Be careful to use a small flame and do not overheat as methylated spirits boils at a low temperature and may ignite. If this happens simply cover the tin cutting off the air supply and so quenching the flame. Do not under any circumstances pour water on the burning spirits or touch it. Methylated spirits will damage turquoise, opal, pearl and other soft absorbent stones. Shellac can also be removed from the metal mounts by careful chipping and scraping with a flat scorper leaving only a thin residue which can be wiped off with a cloth dampened in methylated spirits or dissolved by a short dip in the cold liquid.

Another very useful implement is a wax stick, ideal for picking up stones cleanly and more efficiently than with the hands. It is made from a piece of beeswax mixed with a little soot or plaster of Paris to reduce the tackiness of the wax.

Burnished Settings

A burnished setting is a simple band of metal surrounding a stone. The metal is pushed and finally polished by burnishing over the edge of the stone. In its simplest form it is suitable for fairly large cabochon stones and delicate stones such as opals, turquoise, and cameos. I would suggest beginning with a fairly tough cabochon stone such as garnet, cornelian, or quartz, about 15–20mm in diameter. Illus 110 shows how to make it.

To set the stone it must first be placed in position to see how much metal needs to be trimmed off the thin outer bezel. High, almost vertical-sided stones need to be set more deeply, the metal coming well up over the sides. Shallow ones with a sharp angled edge are much easier to set. The bezel edge should be trimmed with a small pair of sharp shears (see Chapter 3, Illus 72) until just enough metal is left to press over the edge of the stone and hold it

18ct gold and diamond necklace with detachable front piece which becomes a brooch, together with a matching bracelet, designed and made by Hamish Bowie

Illus 105   Shellac stick and scorpers

Illus 106   Sharpening bull stick and scorpers:
The bull stick is sharpened by firstly grinding away a portion of the side shown in (a) on a power or hand driven grinding wheel. Cool the steel frequently in water during the operation or it will be softened and spoiled. The side of the bull stick is used for opening out holes and settings to take stones and it is sharpened on a fine oil stone to produce the cutting edge shown in (b) and (c). Scorpers are firstly ground as in (d) using the circumference of the grind wheel to give the radius indicated. The front edge is sharpened as a chisel on a fine oil stone. (e), (f) and (g) show flat, half round and spit stick all sharpened in the same way.

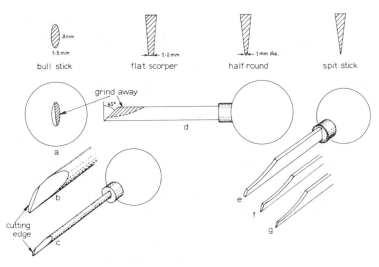

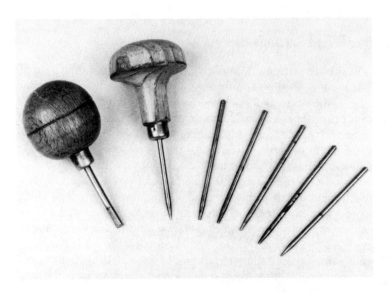

Illus 107   Pusher and graining tools

Methylated spirit

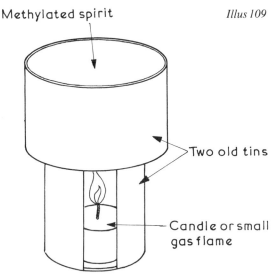

Two old tins

Candle or small
gas flame

securely. It is then worked with a smooth flat file before being finished on an emery stick and polished, firmly rubbing with a polished steel burnisher (Illus 111, 112a). Place the stone firmly in position and support the setting against the bench peg. Using the handle of a pair of pliers which has been prepared with fine emery paper, press the thin metal over the edge of the stone, moving the curvature of the handle in a rolling action all the way round the stone until it is secure (Illus 112b, 112c). Polish the setting edge again with the steel burnisher, rubbing backwards and forwards firmly but briskly, lubricating it with a little spittle (Illus 112d). A little rouge on a soft brush may be used to give a final sparkle, but the object of this type of setting is to avoid the use of emery paper, files, and heavy polishing after the stone is set.

Another type of burnished setting is similar in appearance to the one above, but differs in construction. Although it is suitable for small stones and was used a great deal for tiny half-pearls in Victorian jewellery, it is best to begin with a fairly large hard stone. The construction consists of a simple band of fairly heavy gauge metal, either 0.9mm or 1.1mm depending on the size of the stone (the larger the stone the heavier the gauge). The dimensions of the band should be such that when the stone is stood on top the inside edge is slightly within the perimeter of the stone, and the

Illus 110 Burnished setting; a cabochon cut stone; b strip to form outer band of the setting; c thickness; d turn up, solder and fit stone; e strip to form inner band; f thickness; g turn up, solder and fit in outer band; h solder inner band inside outer band; i stone should be an accurate fit

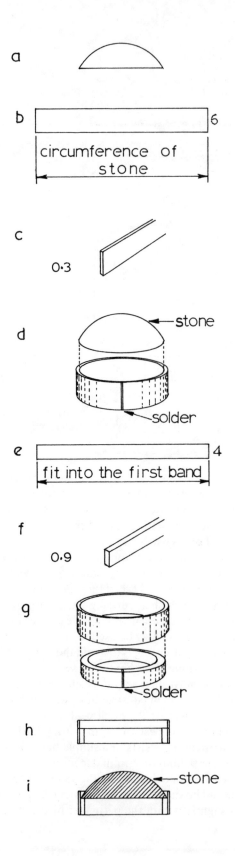

a

b | circumference of stone | 6

c 0·3

d stone solder

e | fit into the first band | 4

f 0·9

g solder

h

i stone

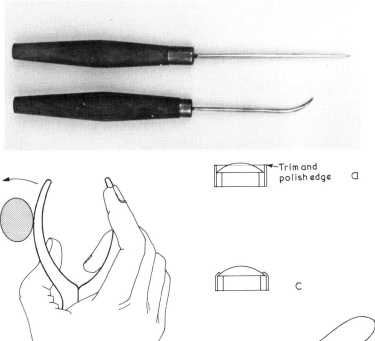

Trim and
polish edge   a

c

b

Illus 112   d

outer edge lies slightly outside (Illus 113). To set the stone a ledge
is cut in the inside top edge of the bezel with a bull stick (Illus 114),
moving the sharp edge of the implement and at the same time
rotating the setting, so that an even amount of metal will be removed from the setting. The cut out ledge should hold the stone
exactly and so it is necessary to check as you cut by frequently
lowering the stone onto the ledge. Sloppiness at this stage will
make further work and finishing very much more difficult. If
everything has been done correctly, the stone should drop into
place neatly with an edge of metal standing round. If the stone
does not settle down properly, make sure the ledge is sufficiently
deep and of the right shape (Illus 113). Do not, as is often the case
with beginners, continue opening out the setting in the hope that
the stone will eventually fit.

Once the stone is sitting properly it is removed, the metal edge is
thinned carefully with a smooth file before replacing the stone and
pressing the metal over the stone with a pusher. Hold the setting
steadily against the bench peg with one hand and firmly grasp the
pusher in the other, nip the metal over the stone at four opposite
points to pin it in position (Illus 115). This is most important if by
any chance the stone is slightly loose fitting. Work round gradually always overlapping the previous movement. This avoids

Illus 113 Burnished setting;
a cabochon cut stone; b strip
to form setting; c thickness;
d turn up and solder; e inside
diameter of setting is smaller
than diameter of stone but
outer diameter is greater;
f with half round file bevel
inside edge to diameter of
stone; g with bull stick cut
recess for stone; h stone should
fit accurately; i alter
proportions for high stones

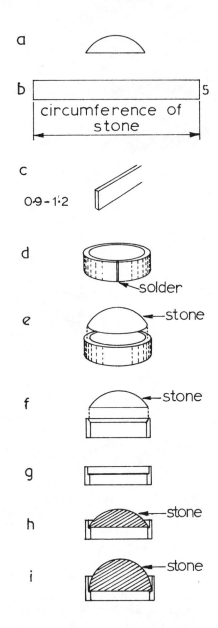

kinking. It may be necessary to go round the circumference two or three times to bring the metal evenly down on the stone. Care should be taken to prevent the pusher from touching the stone at any time for unless you are working with a strong stone it may break.

If the top edge is slightly uneven it can be trued up with a flat scorper held so as just to skim the surface removing the high spots. The action is quick and must not be jerky, nor should the scorper be allowed to dig in by cutting at too steep an angle (Illus 116). Alternatively the marks of the pusher are removed firstly with a needle file which has had the edge ground smooth to give a surface that will not damage the stone (Illus 117), and then with a Water of

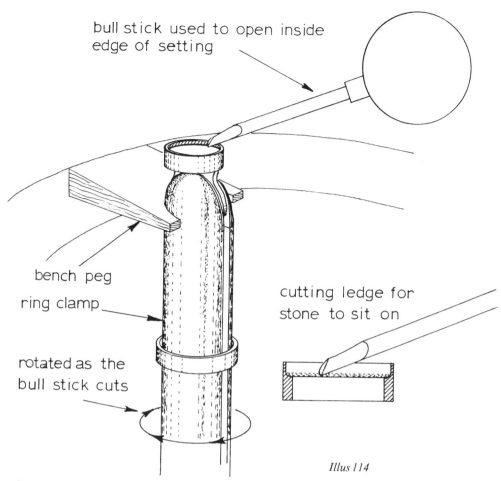

bull stick used to open inside edge of setting

bench peg

ring clamp

rotated as the bull stick cuts

cutting ledge for stone to sit on

Illus 114

Ayre stone and a little water. The surface is then polished with various grades of rouge, using either hand or mechanical processes. At no time must emery paper or carborundum be used for finishing in close proximity to stones as there is a high risk of damage.

Illus 118 and 119 show how a burnished setting can be employed in the making of a ring and pendant.

Claw Settings

There are several conventional types of claw settings, the simplest of which is the four claw. Usually about 4–5mm high it can be made from a strip of metal about 0.7mm thick and 5mm wide. The strip can be pierced out of sheet metal with a radius of about 40mm which is rather a wasteful method and not practical if you are using silver or gold, or it can be bent from a strip using the bending device shown in Illus 120.

The bending jig is held in a vice by the vertical bar (Illus 121). The strip of metal is slipped under the bridge just sufficiently far to be located there. Using a pair of broad flat nose pliers, clamp the strip to the lower washer just in front of the bridge. Then with another pair of flat pliers grip the strip of metal just in front of the

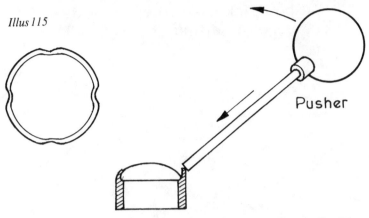

Illus 115

Pusher

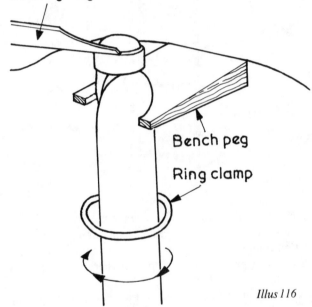

Scorper held at low angle to true bevelled setting edge

Bench peg

Ring clamp

Illus 116

Position and solder one side at a time

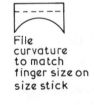

File curvature to match finger size on size stick

Bind with doubled length of binding wire

Edges ground off to give safe edge

Needle file *Illus 117*

Fit setting to size on size stick

Illus 118

74

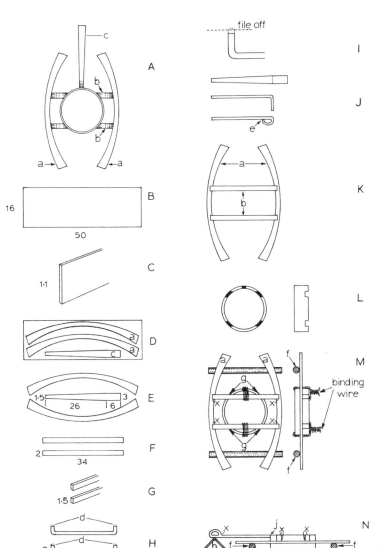

Illus 119 Pendant using a burnished setting. A finished pendant; B parts marked a from sheet metal; C thickness; D outline the components with a scriber; E pierce them out with a jeweller's fret saw; F parts marked b from strip metal; G thickness; H bend as shown, melt HMP solder onto the edges d file bump of solder formed to a flat but do not remove all the solder; I detail; J part c is turned up with a pair of round nose pliers, solder with HMP, solder at e. All parts are now filed true, rubbed down with emery and polished or textured as required. Suggest parts b are heavily textured; K parts a are placed on an asbestos sheet and parts b placed one at a time, fluxed and heated until the solder on them flushes; L recesses for b and c are cut in the back of the setting with a piercing saw and square needle file; M use MMP solder; the setting is bound to the bars with iron binding wire. Steel rods f are positioned to support parts a the solder is put at g and heated. Solder joins marked with an x are painted with a paste of jeweller's rouge before soldering operations; N use LMP solder; c is located in the setting and supported by h – a piece of bent sheet iron – and soldered at j.

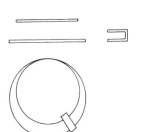

Illus 120

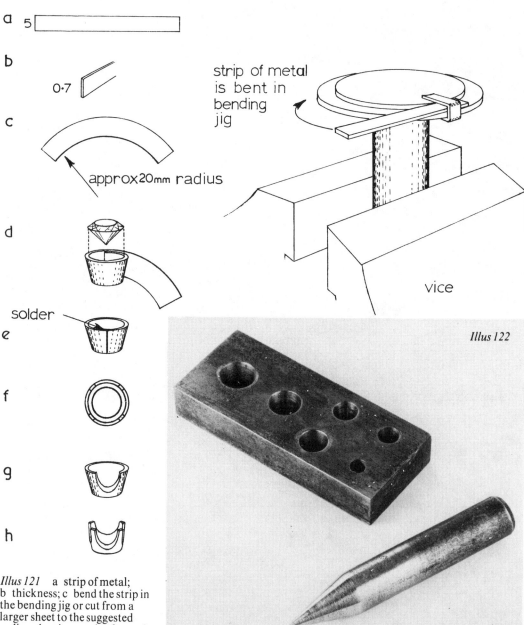

a strip of metal; b 0·7 thickness;

strip of metal is bent in bending jig

c approx 20mm radius

d

solder

e

f

g

h

vice

Illus 122

Illus 121 a strip of metal;
b thickness; c bend the strip in
the bending jig or cut from a
larger sheet to the suggested
radius; d using a pair of round
nose pliers turn up the setting.
The inside diameter at the large
end should be the same as the
stone to be set; e saw the setting
off the remainder of the strip
and solder with HMP solder.
True in the tapered punch and
plate; f divide the top of the
setting into four with a round
needle file; g file the claws out
with a round needle file.
Position the solder line between
the claws; 1 the finished setting
with four strong claws

first pair of pliers and push, forcing the strip to bend round the
central raised washer. Bend only a little at a time gradually feeding
it through the bridge until you have enough length to construct
the settings required. The second and possibly quicker method of
producing a tapered collet is to use a collet plate with a tapered
punch (Illus 122).

More complex claw settings can be tried out after you have
mastered the simpler ones. The claw and organ pipe is a traditional setting, named because its design resembles the end of an
organ pipe. Again for stones up to 6mm in diameter use metal of

0.7mm thickness, larger stones of 12mm diameter require up to 1.1mm thickness. Illus 123 shows how to do it. Large stones can be set in more than eight claws depending on the size of the stone but the principle of construction is the same.

As with the burnished setting the back of the setting should be shaped to suit the role it will fulfil as the base of the setting. If it is to fit against the finger as in a ring then the curvature of the finger in question should be filed into the bezel using a sizing triblet or size stick to ensure the curve is accurate (Illus 118).

Setting a stone in a claw is carried out with a flat scorper cutting down vertically to shave a little metal from the top inside edge of each claw forming a ledge on which the stone must rest (Illus 124).

After the stone is set each claw must be shaped so as to be smooth and for this a three square file with its corners ground smooth is required. Take the sharp edges off the side of each claw and smooth the top of each with the flat scorper drawing the cutting edge backwards over the metal to scrape and burnish the claw to a smooth contour.

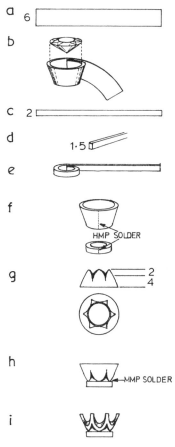

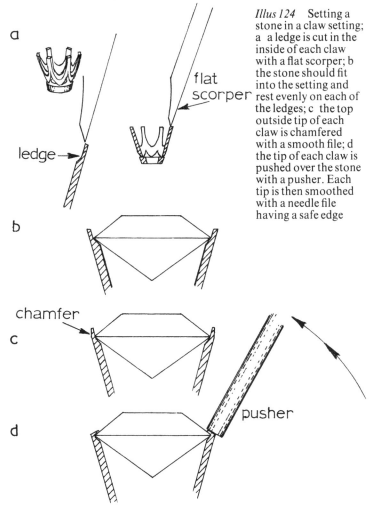

Illus 124 Setting a stone in a claw setting; a a ledge is cut in the inside of each claw with a flat scorper; b the stone should fit into the setting and rest evenly on each of the ledges; c the top outside tip of each claw is chamfered with a smooth file; d the tip of each claw is pushed over the stone with a pusher. Each tip is then smoothed with a needle file having a safe edge

Illus 123 a strip of metal is the same as for the four claw setting but slightly wider; b treat in the same way as for a four claw setting. Adjust the size to suit the stone which should be the same diameter as the top inside edge of the setting; c strip for the back rim of the setting; d thickness; e turn into a circle to fit the bottom of the setting; f the setting is soldered and trued in a tapered punch and plate (Illus 122). The back rim is soldered and trued; g the bottom edge of the setting is divided into six or eight, depending on the number of claws required, with a three square file; h the setting is tied with binding wire to the back rim of the setting and soldered with tiny panels of solder on the points; i the claws are cut with a round needle file to correspond with the divisions in the bottom edge of the setting

77

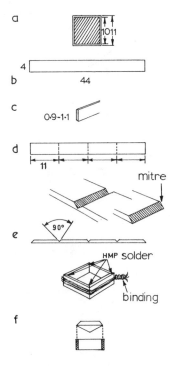

Illus 125 A square parallel setting: a top view of a 10mm square stone in a burnished setting; b strip suitable for the setting of a 10mm stone. The width of this depends on the height required for the stone and is therefore variable; c the thickness of the strip is variable. Small stones can be set in 0.9, larger stones like this one require 1.1 thickness; d the strip is divided into four with a square needle file which should cut a 90°V threequarters of the way through the strip. The two ends should be mitred at 45°; e the strip is bent up into an open-ended box. It is bound with a double length of iron binding wire and soldered at each corner with HMP solder; f the stone should be slightly larger than the inside of the setting. When the stone is placed on the setting the outer perimeter of the setting should be plainly visible around the stone

Square Settings

It is not feasible to construct a burnished setting for a square stone using the double band construction (Illus 110). An open-ended box of fairly heavy wall thickness (0.9 or 1.1mm depending on the size of the stone) should be constructed in strip metal. Stones over 12mm square will require the heavier gauge and the setting can be either straight-sided or tapered. The setting should be deep enough to accommodate the stone (Illus 125).

Generally the setting needs a certain amount of adjustment and squaring up. For this the square end of a small anvil (see Illus 13) is used as a mandrel on which the setting can be trued with the aid of a 4oz hammer. More than likely, one or more of the sides will need stretching and this can easily be done on the anvil using the hammer to stretch the metal.

To make a tapered setting, bend the strip of metal which is to form the setting in the bending machine. The width of this strip is limited to about 8mm because it is not feasible to bend anything wider in the jig. To produce a taller setting it is necessary to pierce the curved strip out of a sheet of metal so as to obviate bending. Illus 126 shows how.

Setting square stones is shown in Illus 127 and 128.

Square claw settings can be constructed by making a collet in the same manner as for a burnished square tapered setting. When cutting claws remember that the corners of square stones need to be held and protected. It is very unsatisfactory to hold a square cut stone by claws in the centre of each side (Illus 128) as this invariably leads to loose stones and leaves the corners totally unprotected. The most vulnerable part of a square or rectangular stone is its corners, so great care has to be taken, particularly with such stones as emeralds, opals, and turquoises, which are fragile at the best of times.

Oval Settings

Tapered round or oval settings can be made using the same techniques as for square tapered settings. The sequence of construction is shown in Illus 129 and the technique of setting in the relevant section. All metal thicknesses are as for the square setting.

Oval claw settings are constructed in the same way as round settings except that unless you make a special oval mandrel there is no other means of truing the setting other than careful manipulation with pliers and hammer. Should the setting be a little small or be insufficiently tapered then it can be stretched by forging with a 4oz hammer on the round end of an anvil (see Illus 13).

Box Settings

This is shown in Illus 130.

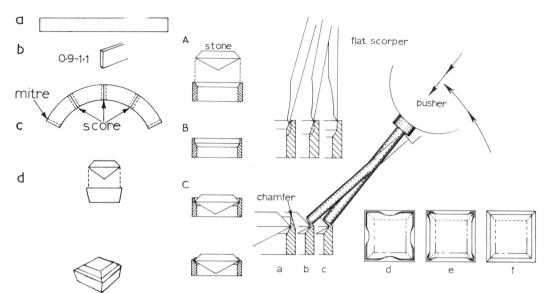

Illus 126 A square tapered setting: a strip as for previous setting; b thickness; c strip is bent in bending jig and scored with a square needle file as previously described; d strip is folded at the scores and soldered as described

Illus 127 Setting a stone in a square setting: A the inside edge of the setting is bevelled out to the perimeter of the stone with a needle file; B the inside edge of the setting is opened out with a flat scorper until the stone fits accurately and settles neatly on the ledge. Care should be taken to ensure that the corners of the stone do not foul the setting for they are easily broken; C the stone is placed in the setting. The outer edge is

thinned by chamfering with a file (a). The pusher is used to press the metal over the stone (b and c). Start by pressing the metal over at the middle of each side (d), work gradually toward the corners (e), finally press the corners down (f) and finish the edge with a smooth file followed by Water of Ayre stone, not emery paper. The edge can then be polished in the normal way

Secure

Not secure

Illus 128

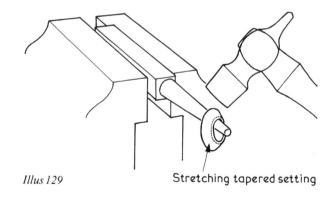

Illus 129   Stretching tapered setting

Illus 130 Box setting: A metal required for the setting of an 8 × 10mm trap cut stone; B thicknesses; C the blank is divided into sixths in its longest dimension given and along its shortest into quarters. From this the shape can be worked out and then cut out with a piercing saw. Score at c-d e-f with a square needle file; D bend at the scores and solder. Solder a and b in position; E turn setting over score with edge of square needle file at g-h and i-j. Bend the two ends down; F bind to a simple 3mm wide band and solder at three points. G Clean and polish and set as shown; when scoring cut deeply with a saw blade across a guide line and then open out with the square needle file cutting a little over half way through the metal

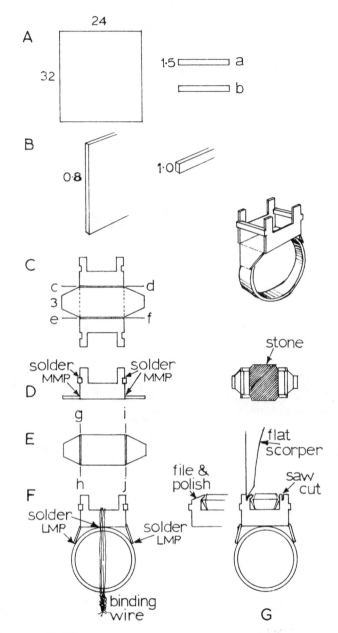

Roman Settings

Roman setting is a form of burnished setting and when properly carried out is very beautiful and most effective. Cabochon stones are sunk into heavy gauge sheet metal (approx 2mm). The stone should sit with its girdle below the surface of the metal and a bull stick is used to open out the hole (Illus 114). It is essential that the stone fits accurately and tightly in position, for unlike other types of burnished settings where you can get away with slight inaccuracies, Roman setting will not work if the stone fits loosely (Illus 131).

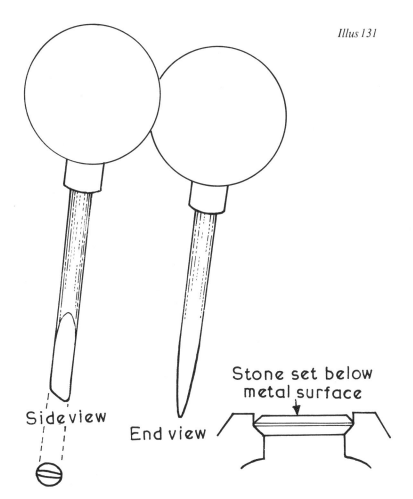

Side view   End view

Stone set below
metal surface

After the stone has been fitted, the next step is to burnish a groove round it using a special burnisher shown in Illus 131. This is applied under pressure to the metal immediately surrounding the stone and at the same time moved around the stone smoothly and firmly, being actually guided by gently touching the stone. The pressure on the metal should be light at first until a groove is formed, and then more heavily applied, but care must be taken that this is put on the metal and not on the stone. Providing that the action of the burnisher is smooth and even all the way round, the result is a deep burnished groove which has displaced the metal over the edge of the stone, so securing it (Illus 132). Any marks caused by the burnisher slipping can be removed with Water of Ayre stone.

Although simple in concept this setting is very exacting in execution.

Pavé Setting

This is a means of setting a mass of round stones in the surface of a piece of metal which has been drilled to accept them (Illus 133).

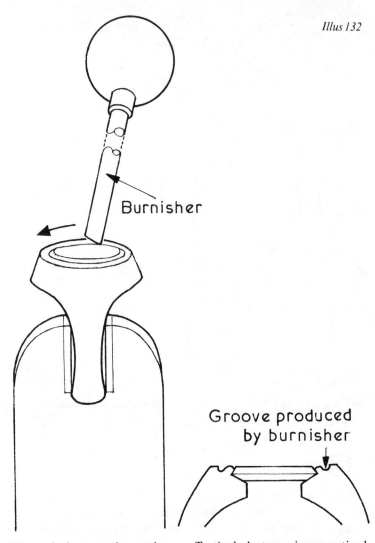

Burnisher

Groove produced
by burnisher

The technique can be used very effectively but requires practised skill. The object is to place the stones as closely together as possible. Before drilling any holes the stones are laid out in position on a piece of plasticine shaped to represent the metal. Measurements can then be taken with dividers to determine the centre of each hole to be drilled. Set the metal in the shellac stick and use a small drill to make the holes initially before opening them out gradually. This gives you the opportunity to correct the positions slightly – essential when you are working with stones of different sizes. The holes are opened out with tapered cutters shown in Illus 134 (available in sets of graduated sizes) until at their largest diameter they are exactly the size of the stone, and the stones set as in Illus 135.

Polishing is done with common whitening block and water made into a fairly thick mixture applied to the setting which is then held against a short haired circular brush on the polishing motor. The beauty of this polishing composition is that unlike the

Silver pendant with rose quartz designed and made by Heather Powell

82

ones consisting of rouge and a greasy binding agent, it is easily washed out of the nooks and crannies of the setting with soap and water and a brush.

Gem Stones

An essential property of a gem stone is hardness, for however beautiful and brilliant a mineral may be it is of little use to the jeweller if it lacks sufficient hardness to withstand the abrasion of everyday use. Brilliant as a glass imitation stone (generally termed paste) may be, in general use it will be rubbed and lose its lustre in a comparatively short time. There is a definite scale of hardness laid down under the name of Mohs's Scale. On it diamond reigns supreme with the arbitrary value of ten, and a remarkable fact is that the difference in hardness between corundum, the second hardest, and diamond is greater than between talc – number 1 on the scale – and corundum. The numbers in the scale do not denote equal degrees of hardness but were arrived at by selecting ten minerals whose hardness was determined by the ability of one to scratch the other and arranged accordingly:

MOHS'S SCALE OF HARDNESS

1	TALC	$6\frac{1}{2}$	IRON-PYRITES
2	GYPSUM	7	QUARTZ
3	CALCITE	$7\frac{1}{2}$	BERYL
4	FLUOR-SPAR	8	TOPAZ
5	APATITE	9	CORUNDUM
6	ORTHOCLASE	10	DIAMOND

Diamond impregnated phosphor bronze discs are used to cut diamond and other gem stones and the finest glass cutters have a diamond cutting edge. It is important when storing any gem stones that they are wrapped individually, for when rubbed together one will scratch the other, even when they are of the same family and hardness.

Jeweller's files will scratch all minerals below a hardness of 6 and talc and gypsum can be scratched with the fingernail. Although a stone may be quite hard it does not mean that it will not break easily and even diamond has lines of cleavage along which it will break. Emeralds and topaz although of hardness value $7\frac{1}{2}$ and 8 respectively are notoriously prone to breaking even under the slightest pressure and great care has to be exercised when dealing with these stones. In the case of emerald, settings are usually made of 22ct gold, platinum or silver, preferably pure silver. These metals are softer than the lower carat qualities of gold, therefore pressure on the setting is less when the stone is being secured which reduces the risk of breakage.

Diamond, ruby and sapphire are very resistant stones and will tolerate the low melting point temperature of 18ct gold solders.

(*Top*) 18ct gold and pavé-set diamond ring designed and made by Susan Whitehead

(*Bottom*) Silver and smokey quartz dress ring designed and made by Hamish Bowie

85

However, they do have to be protected from oxidising agents with a coat of boric acid. Diamond will burn or oxidise if maintained at a temperature of 850°C in air, the boric acid however, increases its ability to withstand even higher temperatures by sealing it from the air.

White spinels, white zircons and to a lesser extent garnet, with the protection of a boric acid coating, can withstand easy (low melting point) silver and gold solders. But the operation should only be carried out if really essential as the risk of damage is high. I have mentioned this point simply because if by chance an item of jewellery you have made does get broken, then very often repairs by soldering can be effected without removing the stones. Do not attempt to heat any stones other than those I have mentioned. When cooling, allow them to do so gradually away from draughts and cold surfaces as sudden cooling will shatter the stone. Gem stones were formed under high temperatures and immense pressures and very often they have flaws or inclusions in the neighbourhood of which there are stresses. An inclusion is a vulnerable point in a stone and before setting it is advisable to examine to establish the whereabouts of these and to avoid pressure on them. Such are the stresses for instance, in a diamond at the inclusions that the spontaneous explosion of the stone has often been observed. The emerald is a stone very prone to flaws and inclusions.

Opal

Opal is extremely fragile and has to be treated with great care as the finer examples are very highly priced. Fine opal is generally set in a burnished setting made of soft metal, ideally 22ct gold, but sometimes platinum or silver. The conditions under which opal is kept are highly critical. It contains between 3 per cent and 12 per cent water so that dry, hot atmospheres can cause dehydration resulting in loss of colour, and sometimes cracking. The opal is a soft mineral of only 5.5 to 6.5 hardness and as most particles of dust have harder constituents abrasion is a serious problem. These stones are not suitable for engagement rings or jewellery which is worn continuously.

The Quartz Family

There is a vast range of stones within this family. They have a reasonable durability and form the majority of stones a jeweller handles (7 on Mohs's Scale). The more important varieties of the family are: agate, amethyst, aventurine, bloodstone, cairngorm, carnelian, cat's eye, chalcedony, chrysoprase, flint, heliotrope, jasper, mocha stone, onyx, rock crystal, sard and sardonyx. The transparent forms have a limited range of colours being either

Illus 133   18ct gold and diamond ring designed and made by Sue Whitehead

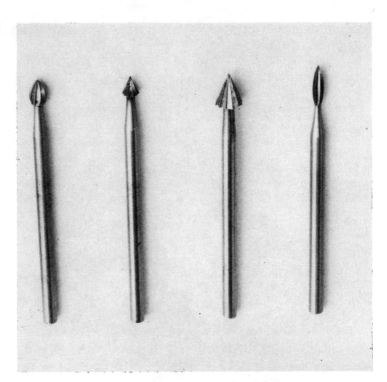

colourless (rock crystal), pink (rose quartz), violet (amethyst), brown (smoky quartz), or yellow (citrine).

Agate

The name agate is applied to a mineral composed of an aggregate of various forms of silica very often laid down in layers. Such agates when cut exhibit a succession of parallel lines giving a banded effect, and are called banded, riband or striped agates. They were usually formed as nodules in ancient lavas where they represent cavities wholly or partially filled with the silica matter. To a lesser extent agate is found in veins and very often contains quartz crystals and amethyst. Sometimes large nodules have been formed with air pockets inside, the inner walls of which are also lined with crystals of quartz and amethyst. Such a formation is called a Geode and like all agates can be of an immense size, examples weighing up to 35 tons have been exhibited.

If the cut agate shows concentric circles due either to stalactic growth or deposits in the form of beads, the stone is known as *eye agate*. Inclusions of green material, usually silicates rich in iron disposed in filaments and other forms suggestive of vegetable growth, form *Moss Agates*.

In the course of time the lava rock containing the agate nodules is broken down, the nodules are set free and because of their extreme resistance to the action of air and water remain as nodules in the soil and gravel, or as rocks and pebbles in rivers and streams. The agates cut and polished today originate mainly from South America where they are found as boulders in river beds.

a

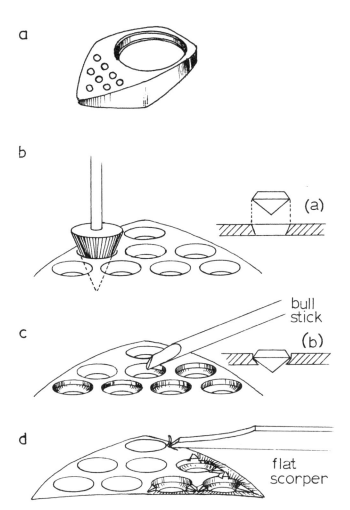

b

(a)

bull
stick

(b)

c

d

flat
scorper

e

half round
scorper

f

graining
tool

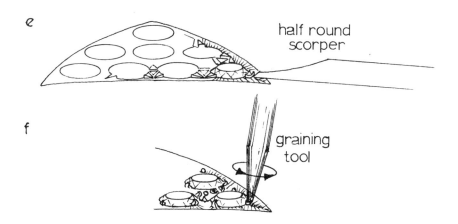

Illus 135 Pavé setting: a the stones are laid out on plasticene in the pattern required. Their positions are measured from centre to centre with dividers and transferred to the surface of the metal which is then drilled with a drill smaller in diameter than the stones; b each hole is opened to a taper with a tapered cutter (Illus 134) which is held in a jeweller's drill, detail (a) shows the required size; c the bull stick is used to fit the stone individually. The girdle of each stone must lie beneath the metal, detail (b); d remove the stones. The flat scorper is used to cut metal away leaving raised triangles around each stone; e the stones are replaced. The half round scorper is used to cut into the raised triangles pushing them over the edge of the stones. It is used to raise the metal between the stones into a mass of spikes; f each spike is converted to a bead using a graining tool. This is a simple hardened steel rod with a handle. The end tapers almost to a point with a small indentation in it. Used under pressure with a rotating waggling action it burnishes the spike of metal into a tiny hemisphere

Stained Agates

Most commercial agates are stained, a process which transforms normally grey uninteresting material into attractive gem stones much sought after for carving, cutting, and polishing. To produce a dark brown or black stone the agate is soaked for two or three weeks in a sugar solution or olive oil at a moderate temperature. The solution is absorbed. The stone is then thoroughly washed and immersed in a dilute solution of sulphuric acid which soaks into the stone carbonising the absorbed sugar or oil making it black. Layers of the agate may not be permeable and may be left as white bands. The resultant stone is called onyx.

When the agate is soaked in a solution of ferrous sulphate for an extended period, then warmed causing the impregnated chemical to turn red, it is known as a carnelian or sardonyx. Some stones found naturally, contain an iron compound which gives them a brown appearance and on baking in the sun this turns to the rich brownish red opaque colour.

Sometimes agate is stained to imitate lapis lazuli, often termed Swiss lapis, by soaking in a solution of an iron salt, either ferrocyanide or ferriccyanide of potassium. Green agate which is called chrysoprase can be produced by soaking in a solution of nickel or chromium salts and a yellow tint can be produced by the action of hydrochloric acid.

Agates make up a fascinating mineral species of infinite variety. They are inexpensive and easily found by the amateur searching areas rich in pebbles of the species such as beaches and old and new river and stream beds where they are found as weathered pebbles.

None of the quartz family can be raised to high temperatures with safety for many of them undergo colour changes or shatter with excessive heat. Most of them are fairly strong although the transparent varieties tend to chip or flake especially at corners and a modicum of care is required particularly in setting when hardened steel implements are used.

Garnet

The garnet is a very popular stone in jewellery mainly because of its pleasant colours, abundance, and reasonable cost. Although it has a hardness of between $6\frac{1}{2}$ and 7 the garnet, like the transparent quartz, has to be carefully handled for excessive setting pressures or the point of the setting tool can chip or flake a piece from the stone, especially at corners.

There are four types of garnet used as gem stones: Almandine, Hessonite, Demantoid and Pyrope. They cover a remarkable range of colours from brownish-red Pyrope and purplish-red Almandine, to orange or brown Hessonite and green Demantoid. This colour range is only roughly laid out for the first two may cross into each of the colours mentioned and in fact both types can be pink. The two types in general use are Pyrope and Almandine as the others are somewhat rarer.

Tourmaline

Tourmalines have probably the greatest variety of colours known in gem stones, ranging from any shade of green, red, pink, dark-blue, mid-blue, yellow, brown, to clear transparent stones. Crystals are found with one colour at one end and another at the other end, going through all shades of the colour in between. It is common to find cut stones which are pink at one end and green at the other with a distinct line of colour change across the middle of the stone. The stone is very often flawed so care has to be exercised when setting for excessive pressure can break a crystal or cut stone in half. Hardness is 7 to $7\frac{1}{2}$.

Lapis Lazuli

Lapis Lazuli is a deep blue opaque stone, very often containing traces of Pyrites in the form of spangles. It is fairly soft stone with a Mohs's scale value of $5\frac{1}{2}$ so care has to be exercised for it can easily be damaged with the file or setting scorper. For this reason it is more suited to the burnished type of setting which affords some protection of the stone.

Zircon

Zircon is another stone which is found in a great variety of colours ranging through red, pink, brown, yellow, green, blue and white. It is subject to colour change with heat and most of the white and blue stones in general use are so treated as a means of improving their appearance. A fairly soft mineral ($6\frac{1}{4}$ Mohs's scale) it is subject to wearing and rubbing of the surface. Do not work near the stone with emery paper which will certainly cause damage, and take care when setting.

Topaz

Coloured Topaz in shades of yellow, blue, green and pink of fine quality are rare, and expensive. Colourless Topaz is the commonest type and is quite inexpensive. With a hardness of 8 it is reasonably durable, but suffers from strong cleavage tendencies which have to be considered with care when setting. Certain brown Topaz can bleach on exposure to sunlight and yellow Topaz when heated will turn pink so that most pink Topaz occurring in jewellery is artificially heated.

Spinel

Vast quantities of synthetic spinel are made and used in the jewellery industry which makes natural stones all the more rare to see. Naturally it is found in colours ranging from deep red, rose red, pink, orange-yellow, purple, blue, grass-green, dark green to black. It is a fine hard mineral (8 Mohs's scale) and raises few problems for the craftsman in setting. In many instances red spinels have been taken for rubies, as they have a great similarity and are often found set in the same piece. The historic Ruby set in the Maltese Cross in the front of the Imperial State crown of

England is a spinel. It was given by Pedro the Cruel, King of Castile, to Edward the Black Prince on the victory of Najera in 1367.

Corundum

A fine hard mineral (9 Mohs's scale) which occurs in a range of colours. Red is known as ruby. Blue, colourless, yellow, pink. Green, purple and violet stones are all known as sapphire. Star sapphire and ruby show asterism in the form of a six rayed star. Corundum is a very resistant material most suitable for every day use, such as in engagement rings, and with certain precautions

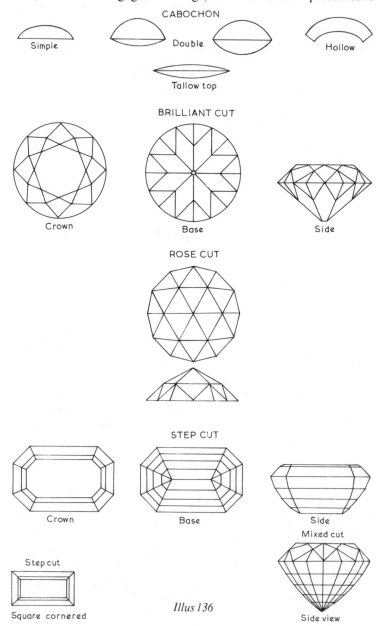

CABOCHON

Simple   Double   Hollow

Tallow top

BRILLIANT CUT

Crown   Base   Side

ROSE CUT

STEP CUT

Crown   Base   Side

Mixed cut

Step cut

Square cornered

Illus 136

Side view

92

they will withstand high temperatures. Care should be taken when trimming claw or other types of setting with a file, to see that there is a safe edge ground on the file to avoid the risk of chipping the edge of the stone. (See Illus 117). This applies to all stones but very often one tends to consider the more resistant minerals as indestructible, a mistaken concept for all must be treated with the utmost care.

Diamond

This is the hardest mineral known to man (Mohs's scale 10) and also the most brilliant when faceted. Its physical and chemical properties have been the object of a great deal of study in view of the difference in physical properties of the diamond and those of graphite and charcoal to which it is chemically identical and to which it can be converted by the action of heat or electricity.

Cloudy and faintly coloured specimens are more common than absolutely colourless stones. Usually they are found in tints of grey, brown, yellow, or white, although rare specimens have been found coloured red, pink, green, blue, and black. Artificial colouring can be brought about by irradiation. Although hard and often considered imperishable diamond has the property of perfect cleavage so that care in setting is important. Sometimes the edge of a large stone may be chipped through an inadvertant blow against a sharp hard edge, so that even the most durable mineral has to be treated with a modicum of care. The most famous of the coloured diamonds is the Hope blue diamond of $44\frac{1}{4}$ carats. It is a beautiful blue brilliant considered to be part of a brilliant of $67\frac{2}{16}$ carats, stolen from the French crown jewels, which was originally cut from a rough stone weighing $112\frac{3}{16}$ carats. In 1905 the largest known diamond was found at the Premier mine in the Transvaal. This extraordinary diamond weighed $3025\frac{1}{4}$ carats ($1\frac{1}{3}$ lb) and was clear and white like water. One surface appeared to be a cleavage plane so that it may be only a portion of a much larger stone. It was named the Cullinan Diamond and in 1908 it was cut into nine larger stones and several small brilliants. The largest of these is a flawless brilliant of the finest quality weighing $516\frac{1}{2}$ carats, the largest brilliant in existence.

Cuts of Stones

The jeweller can choose from a selection of standard types of stone shapes and cuts (Illus 136) and if he has the facilities may cut his own stones to any shape required.

Cabochon

Stones cut in this manner are perfectly smooth convex carbuncles which have a flat or even a concave back. Usually in plan they are round or oval but may also be square, rectangular, cushion, triangular or any other shape. They have a high, medium or shallow dome.

The Brilliant Cut

The brilliant cut is a facetted style designed specially to give maximum reflection from a stone which is generally round but it can also be applied to Marquise and other shapes. Designed for the diamond the number of facets should be fifty-eight with thirty-three above the girdle and twenty-five below. In the case of older stones there is often a facet on the base of the stone making fifty-nine. This is called a cullet and is avoided in modern stones as it is detrimental to the effect of the brilliant cut.

Rose Cut

This cut is applied to low quality diamonds and pyrope garnets but is generally only found in old jewellery. The stone is cut with a flat base and triangular facets either twelve or twenty-four terminating in a point.

Step Trap or Emerald Cut

These are names given to stones which in plan are usually square, oblong (baguette), or octagonal. They are cut with rectangular facets running parallel to the girdle. This type of cut can be applied to an infinite variety of outline shapes.

Weighing Stones

Gem stones are weighed in carats and fractions of a carat which when applied to gold is a reference to quality but not weight.

6 Applied Decoration

There are many techniques used to produce decoration on metal. This chapter deals with enamelling, engraving, and etching. Enamel is applied colour decoration, engraving and etching are processes involving the controlled removal of metal to achieve a decorative surface. They are all processes that can be carried out with simple inexpensive equipment which the novice can easily handle in the home workshop.

Illus 137

Enamelling

Enamelling is a technique that has been used since the fifth century BC to embellish metals and has flourished through the ages. In jewellery it is invaluable to enhance precious metals. It is a coloured glass applied in a granular form and melted onto metal to give a hard glazed surface of pure brilliant colour. Generally used to fill recesses in the metal it may be combined with wire as decoration on the surface of the metal. Laid as a thick ground colour it can have decoration painted onto its surface using very finely ground enamel mixed with oil. After applying with a paint brush it is heated in the kiln until it melts and fuses onto the base enamel. Called painted enamel it is a very thin layer decorating the surface of the thick layer and can be very beautiful as shown by miniatures and decorative panels produced by the French enamellers of the eighteenth and nineteenth century.

As a means of incorporating colour in jewellery enamelling is one of the most important processes available. The vast range of colours and the many techniques that may be used to incorporate enamel make it important from a creative point of view. As colour combinations affect what an item may be worn with this is one process which can be directly influenced by fashion.

Equipment

The equipment required for enamelling is relatively simple and those items shown in Illus 137 and 138 will cover most operations apart from painting enamels. Enamels may be bought in either solid lump form or ready ground. Lump will keep better than ground over long periods but it has to be broken down and ground with a pestle mortar to a fine granular form like castor sugar. This is a tedious operation and ready ground enamels, available in a wide range of colours, save a lot of time and in general are to be recommended. Small shallow crock or glass dishes are necessary to contain the enamel when in use and flat spatulae are necessary to apply the enamels. These may be either bought or made from flat metal. Iron gauze and sheet iron are used to make stands on which to put the enamelled piece when in the firing kiln. Several types of stand may be bought but the homemade ones are quite good enough. Carborundum stones are required for grinding the enamel after firing to achieve an even surface.

The kiln in Illus 138 is a simple hot plate with a lid and is good enough for the size of most jewellery items. Large objects such as box lids or bowls require even heat on all sides, necessitating a proper kiln with heating elements all the way round.

Objects that are to be enamelled should have all soldering completed before firing in the kiln. A special enamelling solder (available for silver and the carat golds and with a high melting point) should be used. All solder joins should be painted with a paste of powdered jeweller's rouge and water or loam and water to prevent the solder melting.

There are four types of enamel made commercially, opaque, transparent, opalescent, and painting enamels. Opaque enamels are dense colours whereas the transparent ones allow light to pass through. Opalescent are transparent but with a cloudy or milky appearance. The effect is irridescent like that of an opal. They are rarely used and require great accuracy in firing if the desired quality is to be achieved. Examples can be seen in many of the finer French pieces of the fifteenth and sixteenth centuries, and more often in the English pieces of the latter end of the eighteenth century.

In the manufacture of enamel the procedure follows this outline. The transparent uncoloured glass is termed flux and to this a variety of oxides of metals are added, each oxide producing a different colour range controlled by the quantity of oxide or by the combination of oxides added. For instance cobalt blue is achieved by adding black oxide of cobalt to powdered flint glass to make a transparent enamel. By adding oxides of copper various shades of green are produced, from turquoise to grass green. Gold oxide is used to produce both transparent and opaque red enamels. The following colours are made by using the appropriate oxides:

platinum – soft greys
uranium and antimony – yellows
manganese – purple
tin – white
iridium – rich black

Opalescent enamels are made in the same way but with the addition of tin oxide which produces the opacity.

Characteristics of Some Enamels
Black: for general purposes dense black is most satisfactory. It is essential to wash it carefully. If fired

more than two or three times without laying down a fresh layer of enamel it tends to degenerate, leaving a dull, unattractive surface. Never submit to a strong acid pickle vat for cleansing as it is not acid proof.

White: it is widely used by jewellers for watch dials. The hard dial opaque white can be applied in a paper thin coat and still retain its opacity at a high temperature. For silver work a special white called 'soft for silver' is advisable in order to avoid the discolouration which often occurs. If soft opaque white is thinly applied over copper, an effective bluish green colouration will appear.

Grey: all greys tend towards pitting. Transparent grey whether it is light, dark, or blue-grey, is one of the best colours over copper. Not enough of the warmth of the copper colour shows through to destroy the neutral tones. On silver transparent greys are even more interesting.

Flux: being a truly transparent colour, flux will reveal any discolouration or flaw which might be on the metal. Soft flux used as a ground coating on copper will remain in place and not bubble up through the top layer of enamel if it is applied in a thin coat. It is essential to use it as an undercoat on copper before applying transparent and red enamels.

Blue: the darker shades of opaque blue are excellent for backgrounds and counter enamel. They adhere to the metal with very little cracking or bubbling. They are permanent and the harder varieties are not affected by acid. On the whole blue is the easiest colour to use. Too thin applications will not give good results when working on copper. This is because copper is a warm coloured metal whereas blue is a cold colour so tends to be neutralised by it. Therefore it is a good plan to apply the first coat of transparent blue a bit heavier than one would with other transparents.

Green: to some extent the transparent greens are also affected by the warm tone of copper and should be handled in the same way as the blues. There are special transparent greens for silver, but the greens for copper such as shamrock and emerald, are sufficiently brilliant on silver. Opaque greens are inclined to be troublesome as colour may be affected by overfiring.

Brown: all the transparent browns and tans are stable in their colour retention. Over copper they give a pinkish tan effect.

Red: both transparent and opaque red enamels seem to

be more problematic than most other colours. Being coloured by the oxide of gold, the reds are exceedingly soft and tend to burn out. Opaque reds, vermilions, and oranges will disappear in high temperatures and require second coats. Care must be taken to keep reds scrupulously clean. An idiosyncracy of opaque red is the black edge which it creates next to another enamel, sometimes this can be very effective.

Purple: opaque purples and lavenders compounded from the oxide of manganese are not common. There are, however, several very beautiful transparent purples. They are successful over copper and gold, but many of them turn a decided shade of green when applied over silver.

Yellow: yellow fired over copper is one of the most exciting colours. Occasionally on copper the transparent yellow may turn to a dull muddy finish.

Ivory: the ivory and cream colours are sold as opaques and are soft, low fire colours. A dark transparent enamel dusted onto the ivory background before placing it in the kiln will flatter the design.

Preparing Enamels

Small lumps should be ground in water to a fine granular form like sugar in a pestle and mortar (Illus 137). The granules must then be washed thoroughly. This is very important whether the enamel is bought ready ground or not. Put the ground enamel in a bowl and flood with water. The impurities will float to the surface in the form of enamel dust which can be poured off. The heavy clean enamel will remain on the bottom and should be rinsed several times to ensure cleanliness, especially when dealing with with transparent, dark, and black opaque colours. The enamel is kept damp ready for use.

Applying Enamel

Enamel may be applied by two methods: dusting dry ground enamel through a fine mesh sieve, or applying damp ground enamel with a spatula. To dust the enamel on to the metal use a fine mesh sieve (Illus 139) which can be bought ready made or made from an old tin with fine brass gauze soldered in the bottom. Place the enamel in the sieve and holding it about 120mm above the object, tap the side of the sieve with a finger so depositing a quantity of enamel. Repeat this process until the metal is covered by an even coating of enamel. It is best to do this over a sheet of clean paper so that the excess powder can be swept up and used again. The object is then carefully placed on an iron gauze stand and very gently set in the kiln to fire.

Wet ground enamel should be applied using a spatula which can either be bought or made by flattening out a piece of copper

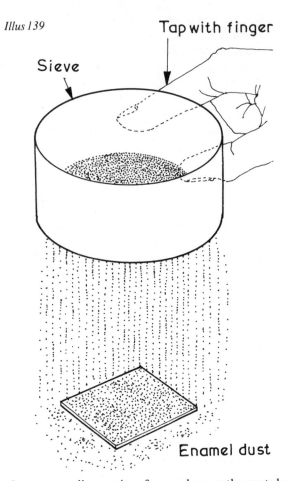

Illus 139

Tap with finger

Sieve

Enamel dust

wire. Scoop a small quantity of enamel up on the spatula carefully draining excess water. Place the enamel in the appropriate areas evenly prodding and pressing it into awkward corners, and finally tap the edge of the object a few times with the spatula. This will cause the enamel to settle and smooth out. Excessive water can be soaked up with a piece of blotting paper. Place the piece on an iron gauze stand and gently warm it above or in front of the kiln until all the water has evaporated. It can then be placed in the kiln for firing. Sudden heating and quick evaporation will cause the enamel to flick off as the moisture boils.

Firing

Switch the firing kiln on and give it time to come up to 750° – 800°C. When the ground enamel has been applied the jewellery piece is then carefully placed on a gauze or sheet iron stand. Using a piece of flat sheet iron with some type of handle the stand and object are taken to the kiln. If the enamel has been packed wet it must be warmed gently over or under the hot kiln until the water has evaporated. Rapid drying brought about by heating quickly causes the water to boil disturbing the enamel and will cause irregularities of the surface when firing is complete. When dry the

jewellery piece is placed in the kiln on its stand (Illus 140). Enamel which is powdered onto the metal dry may be placed in the kiln direct. When in the kiln the surface of the enamel must be observed attentively by peering through the special observation window. This affords a view across the surface of the enamel so that it is easy to see the changing appearance of the enamel up to the point when it has glazed. On the approach to firing temperature the surface will appear to go black then as the enamel granules fuse the surface will become shiny at which point it is removed from the kiln and examined. If it has fired properly the surface should present an even glassy appearance, if it is granular then it needs a little longer in the kiln. It is important not to over fire the enamel and it is better to remove it too soon to see what is happening rather than leave it in too long and spoil the enamel. This especially applies to red and opaque green enamels which can be spoiled by over firing. Opalescent enamels are particularly sensitive and must not be over fired or they will change colour.

The hot enamel piece must be cooled gently after removing from the kiln. Do not place on a cold surface like steel or tile but place it complete with stand either beneath or on top of the hot kiln where it is warm. Such is the stress in enamel when fired onto metal that cracking and chipping can occur with a small temperature change, say from warm hand temperature to being cooled in cold running tap water.

With objects where a counter enamel is used the stand for the object should be made to support the edge of the enamel piece at three or four points so as not to interfere with the counter enamel when it is being fired (Illus 141).

Small simple enamel pieces may be fired over a gas soldering torch. The procedure is to place the piece on a sheet of iron gauze and heat from beneath until the enamel fuses (Illus 142). Do not direct the flame onto the surface of the enamel or it will spoil.

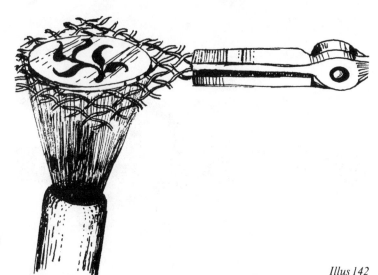

Counter Enamelling

Where large areas of enamel are applied to a relatively thin sheet of metal it is necessary to enamel the other side to control chipping or cracking caused by the difference in the rates of expansion and contraction of the metal and the enamel. Using any left over ground enamels, mix them with a little quantity of gum tragacanth or cellulose wallpaper adhesive. Apply this mixture to the back of the object in an even coating about 1.0mm thick, leave a margin about 2mm wide all around the edge, and dry it gently on top of the kiln. The gum will bind the enamel together making it possible to turn the object over and decorate the front while it is standing on the special stand made to support the edge, shown in Illus 141. If using opaque enamels to decorate an object, apply the counter enamel as thinly as possible, but for the opaques use a heavier backing layer.

Stencilling

Once the enamel has been fired it is possible to apply decoration using a cartridge paper stencil. Simply cut out a shape in a piece of paper and lay this firmly on the enamelled surface. Using the sieve as before, deposit enamel powder onto the stencil which should then be carefully removed. The object is then fired in the kiln and the processes repeated again if desired.

Cloisonné

This enamelling technique which creates a very decorative effect using wire to form enclosed spaces into which different coloured enamels can be fused.

There are three methods of constructing the base for cloisonné. The first is to use a thin sheet of copper or silver about 0.4mm thick and bend the edges up on a steel former about 2mm all the way round (Illus 143a) to form a try. The second is to carve a recess in thick metal (1.3–1.7mm thickness) as shown in Illus

143b. The third way is to use a fairly thick piece of metal (1.2mm thick) and enamel directly onto it. The back of the piece should be counter enamelled. The front coated with a perfectly even thin layer of flux, and fired. The enamel should be unbroken, but if there is a defect, it should be cleaned out with a point, patched with flux and fired again. The top side of the metal will have oxidised during the firing and this must be cleaned off with a stiff brush and pumice or salt and a little water. A less preferable cleaning method is to pickle the object by briefly submerging it in hot sulphuric acid before scrubbing with pumice or salt.

The wires can be strips of 0.4mm metal cut from a thin sheet about 1.5mm wide, or thin round wire which has been rolled flat to give a rectangular section. They are shaped and cut to size (Illus 143c). Having worked out the positioning they are removed and the flux enamelled surface freed from any finger grease by a light scrub with pumice and a brush and then dried. A thin layer of gum tragacanth, cellulose wallpaper paste or ready-made adhesive is painted on to the surface of the flux and the wire cloisons are positioned as required. The object is gently warmed so that the adhesive sets but does not bubble and spoil the positioning of the wires. The next stage is to carefully fire the wires into the flux. If, as is often the case, some of the wires do not fuse into the flux properly, very carefully draw the object to the edge of the kiln and very quickly press the wire down into the flux with a steel blade before it has time to harden, and then re-fire. The cloisons can be soldered into place before any enamel is applied, but this practice is not really desirable, especially when transparent enamels are to be used.

The wire and surfaces should be cleaned as before and are then ready for enamelling. Each colour is placed in its respective cloison with a small spreader and sharp pointer (Illus 143d). The damp enamels must be forced into the tiny spaces making sure that no air bubbles are left. The excess moisture is soaked up with blotting paper and the piece gently warmed to completely dry it out before firing.

Illus 143

Metal former

a

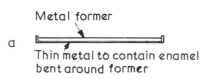

Thin metal to contain enamel
bent around former

Carved out for enamel

Laying cloisons into recess

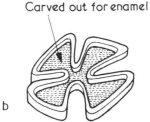

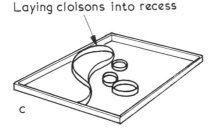

Damp enamel

Spatula

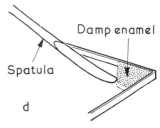

b

c

d

When the first firing is completed the enamels will have shrunk and dip down in the middle so that they seem to be clinging to the wire. A second and possibly third layer of enamel is needed to bring the surface up to the required level. After these firings have been done stone the enamel down to the level of the wire with a carborundum stone under running water. Work gently and evenly over the whole surface until it is perfectly smooth and level. It is now given a final firing to glaze the ground surface. It is essential that the enamel is not overheated during this operation. Watch it until it just becomes glassy and then remove it from the kiln allowing it to cool slowly to avoid cracking and chipping.

Champlevé

A fairly heavy gauge of metal (1.3mm to 1.7mm) is used for this technique. Recesses to hold enamel are either carved or gouged out with scorpers (see page 109), or etched out with acid (see page 110). So long as the areas to be enamelled are not deeper than half the depth of the metal (the ideal depth is about one third of the thickness), it is unnecessary to counter enamel on the back. The enamels are applied to the recessed areas until level with the metal. The whole surface is then stoned under water with carborundum stone until the metal and the enamel are both even. The enamel is fired to glaze as for cloisonné. Illus 144 shows a brooch with enamel areas achieved by soldering a saw pierced design to a back plate with enamelling solder.

Pliqué à Jour

This is the name given to a technique in which open pierced, or fili-gree work is filled with transparent colours and fired. The effect is that of tiny stained glass windows. Before trying pliqué à jour, the function of the finished object must be considered as it has to be viewed or worn so that light penetrates it from either side to get the full effect.

One method is to pierce a design out in sheet metal and place it on a sheet of mica. The holes are filled with enamel and the work suspended on an improvised stand, platform, or prongs, and just enough heat to fire the enamel applied. The mica can then be removed. If the mica becomes fused to the enamel by high firing temperatures then the back must be stoned with carborundum under water and the object fired again.

Another method is to build up filigree wire work and solder it to a plate of thin copper. The enamels are fired in place and then by covering up the enamel and filigree work with asphalt, paint, or some other acid resistant, the back plate of copper can be dissolved in nitric acid (1 part acid to 3 parts water).

The third method is to control the size of apertures so that the enamel remains in place by capillary attraction. Generally these spaces are drilled or pierced in sheet instead of being formed with wire. Each enamel colour is mixed with gum tragacanth, cellulose wallpaper paste, or special adhesive, and placed in the openings

with a spreader. The adhesive and enamel are gently dried over the kiln before firing, which should be carried out on an appropriate wire or gauze stand.

Basse Taille Process

This is simply enamelling over a carved metal surface using transparent enamels.

Problems that Occur

Blemishes can be caused by deposits of the carborundum grinding stone in the enamel. It is a good idea to dip the enamelled object in concentrated hydrofluoric acid for about ten seconds, which will slightly etch the surface releasing the contaminents. It should then be swilled in bicarbonate of soda and water to neutralise any acid, and fired. Unfortunately hydrofluoric acid is extremely dangerous and must not be allowed on the skin, nor should the fumes be inhaled. Keep the bicarbonate of soda always at hand to neutralise and should any acid get on the skin go immediately to get treatment. Always use a plastic container to hold the acid as it dissolves glass. Indeed it is very useful to remove enamel which has to be reapplied. The acid will eat the enamel away fairly quickly but a white resistant deposit builds up slowing down the action and has to be scraped off frequently.

Cracking and chipping on cooling is usually due to insufficient counter enamel, too thick a layer of enamel in relation to metal thickness, or through cooling too rapidly.

Discolouration of enamel, particularly at the edges, is due to too high a temperature or too prolonged firing. Red opaque enamels should receive as few firings as possible for they degenerate and produce black spots on the surface, about which nothing can be done.

Engraving and Carving

Although engraving is a specialisation which takes many years of training and practice, simple textures and carvings can be picked up by the jeweller once he knows how to sharpen and use the appropriate tools. The ring shown in Illus 145 has a simple engraved linear texture on its side surfaces.

Marking Out

Any pattern requiring definite guide lines for engraving or carving can be worked out on paper and transferred to the metal surface. The surface is first painted with a thick coat of Chinese white, or better still, a coat of Gambouge powder mixed into a thin solution with methylated spirits, and allowed to dry. An accurate tracing of the design is made and the reverse side is rubbed over with a soft pencil. The tracing paper is then turned the right way up and placed on the painted metal and the pattern gone round with a hard sharp pencil so transferring it. A sharp steel scriber is used to scratch the design through the paint on to the surface of the metal following the guide line of the pencil. The paint can then be washed off with water leaving the inscribed outline. This method is much more accurate than using glued paper outlines, especially when saw piercing.

The graver is the principal instrument and has a fitted handle similar to the ones used for scorpers. It is square in section and ground on three faces (Illus 146) these being the angled sloping face, and the two bottom faces. The grinding is carried out initially on a well lubricated carborundum oil stone, and then on an oiled Arkansas stone to put the fine cutting edge required on to the steel. To test the sharpness of the point and cutting faces, test on a finger nail. If it slides over the surface of the nail then it is not sharp enough. If it digs in then it should be correct. The ground surfaces should be brightened with a piece of 4/O emery paper on a flat surface if a bright polished cut is required. Test the sharpness

Illus 145   Ring showing linear texture on side surfaces, designed and made by Hamish Bowie

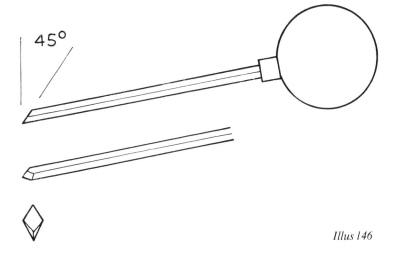

45°

Illus 146

again, for the polishing, if poorly carried out, will make the edge blunt.

It will be helpful to practise engraving on a piece of copper sheet approximately 0.9mm thick and about 60mm square, fastened to a block of wood 100mm square by 12mm thick. The best way of attaching copper to wood is by pouring a thin layer of molten pitch on to the wood and setting in place the slightly warmed sheet. The block is then put on a sand-filled leather bag as support. The graver is held with the thumb running down the side of it while the forefinger runs down the centre line of the graver to steady and control it. To start with try a few straight lines and then progress to cutting circles in one continuous cut. (It will be necessary to scribe guide lines on the metal using dividers or a scriber). The point produces an ordinary V cut but when angled over to one side or the other it will produce broader cuts as the side shaves off more metal. By increasing the angle in relation to the metal the graver will cut deeper. With practice you will learn to control the tool and engrave textures and patterns of a simple nature. The pitch is removed by gentle warming and the remaining traces dissolved by soaking or rubbing with a rag soaked in mineral napthalene.

Lettering is a highly specialised job, so let it suffice to say that those who can do it really well are very few in number and are in great demand. However much decorative work can be carried out using the variety of scorpers which are also used for stone setting (Illus 147). The flat scorper should have its cutting surfaces carefully polished on 4/O emery paper, and can be used to produce broad bright slices in the metal, or wiggled and walked over the surface to make a zig-zag pattern. The various sizes of half round scorpers and spit-sticks can be experimented with to give differing cuts and effects. The shading tool (Illus 148) is a flat scorper with tiny grooves to give a linear texture cut in the under surface. It can be used in one direction only, and is criss-crossed to give other effects, or walked over the surface of the metal like the flat scorper to give a different zig-zag pattern.

Hardening and Tempering of Scorpers and Gravers

Gravers and scorpers are usually bought in the hardened state and in general this condition is suitable for most light work. However, for deep carving and heavy engraving it is necessary to temper or slightly soften the steel so that it does not break. Do this by warming the scorper near the handle end in a flame until the cutting tip reaches a brownish yellow colour when it must be immediately quenched in water. Should scorpers be bought in the soft state

Bull stick

Half-round

Flat

Spit stick

Graver

Illus 147

then it will be necessary to harden the steel by bringing it to a cherry red heat in a flame and quenching it immediately in a bucket of cold water. It is then de-scaled and brightened with emery paper prior to tempering.

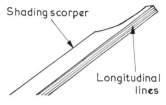

Carving

Carving for Champlevé enamel work is carried out following an inscribed guide line, using a flat scorper sharpened in the manner shown in Illus 149. This angling of the under surface allows the scorper to be used at a steeper angle than normal making it easier to cut out recesses without fouling the edges. As with engraving it is important to fasten the object being worked securely to a wooden block and support it with a sand-filled leather bag. The scorper is wriggled over the metal and worked in a spiral towards the centre of the line so that the same amount of metal is removed from the whole of the surface. This procedure is carried out several times until the required depth is achieved. The surface is then smoothed by straight cutting, scraping strokes of the scorper, or textured to form a feature under transparent enamels. The vertical edges and corners are squared and cleaned up with the spitstick.

Another use of carving is to pierce a design in heavy gauge metal (1.3mm +) and give it three dimensional form by modelling with scorpers. Textures can be applied to give contrasts (Illus 150). Practice, experimentation, and familiarity of the use of cutting tools, all go towards proficiency and versatility.

Illus 149

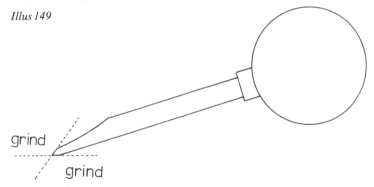

Illus 150 Carved silver bracelet designed and made by Sara Lloyd-Morris

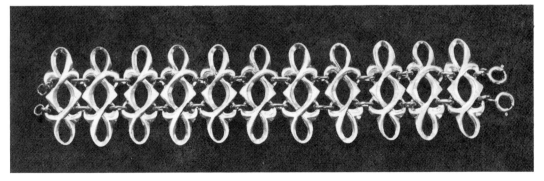

Etching

Etching is a process applicable to most metals. It requires a solution which will dissolve the metal in question and a paint resistant to the action of the solution. It is important that the metal is degreased before anything else is done. Beeswax can be used as a resistant, but for most purposes a good asphaltum varnish (bituminous paint) is suitable and should be coated on all surfaces to be exposed to the solution and scraped off the areas that are to be etched. Alternatively it can be painted only on the areas not being etched, after the design has been marked out on the metal. Once the paint is dry the object is held in a pair of copper tongs in the solution and the surface frequently brushed with a feather to remove a resistant build up that occurs with the action. If this is not carried out the etching will be uneven. Check from time to time to observe the depth of the etch until the required result is achieved. After immersion the object must be swilled well in cold water. The resistant paint is removed after etching with a suitable solvent, such as mineral napthalene.

Different levels can be etched out as in the panels in Illus 151. First etch to one level, say 0.2mm, then paint those areas to be left at that depth and etch again to another level.

Different metals require different dissolving solutions and the formulae below are a rough guide. Correct strengths are worked out by trial. The metal should show a gentle stream of bubbles coming from it. Too much fizzing and bubbling means the solution is too strong; no bubbles means it is too weak. Solutions should always be mixed in a Pyrex bowl ACIDS TO WATER.

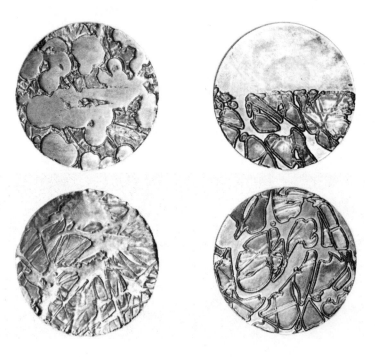

Illus 151

Gold:
(a) Aqua Regia (equal parts of nitric acid and hydrochloric acid). This is diluted to approximately 1 part acid solution to 1 part water.
(b) In a ten per cent potassium cyanide solution using the plating vat in reverse.

Silver:
(a) Nitric Acid diluted to about 40 parts acid to 60 parts water.
(b) Ten per cent potassium cyanide using the plating vat in reverse.

Copper and Alloys:
(a) 1 part nitric acid to 2 parts water.
(b) Sodium Chlorite 35g/l, Ammonium Hydroxide 100g/l, Ammonium Bicarbonate 120g/l at 20–30°C reversing plating process.

Aluminium:
Iron perchloride and water to suit. This is also suitable for copper and gilding metal and is a very effective agent. Unfortunately it is very poisonous.

Iron:
(a) 1oz iodine, $\frac{1}{2}$DR iron filings, 4fl oz water.
(b) 2 parts hydrochloric acid to 8 parts water.

Electro-etching

This process is carried out using the electro-plating equipment so reference to this is important. (See Chapter 8.)

7 Casting

Casting is one of the most important techniques available for the jeweller. From the time metal was first discovered man has used the process and indeed the first form any metal takes is arrived at by the processes of melting and casting. The jeweller can use the technique to produce a complete object by pouring molten metal into specially prepared moulds. Cuttlefish bone used as a mould is the simplest technique and is extremely useful. There are certain limitations in the fact that detailed delicate objects cannot be cast very successfully due to the cuttlefish burning away and the fact that the only force pushing the metal into the mould is the weight of the metal being poured.

Illus 152 shows a brooch produced by cuttlefish casting, and Illus 153 a ring cast in cuttlefish bone then filed, buffed, and polished.

Intricate castings with a lot of surface detail may be produced using the lost wax casting technique (Illus 154 and 155). Intricate wax models are made in wax. These are positioned in a steel mould frame which is filled with a special investment plaster. When this has set it is heated in a kiln until the wax melts out and

Illus 152

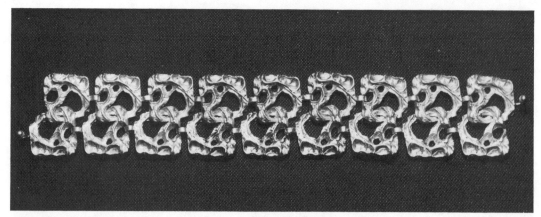

Illus 154 Cast bracelet designed and made by Anthony Perrot

Illus 155 Brooch cast from wax dropped into water by Sylvia Gray

then gradually raised to a temperature of about 700°C. On removal from the kiln the molten metal is forced into the cavity either by steam pressure, centrifugal force, or by using a vacuum to suck it into the mould through the porous investment.

Cuttlefish Casting

The simplest form of casting suitable for all quantities of gold, silver, or brass jewellery work involves the use of a master pattern to make an impression in cuttlefish bone, or simply carving into it. There is a definite procedure to follow if good results are to be obtained.

A cuttlefish bone of good size and depth is sawn in half and the two soft faces flattened off on a sheet of emery paper fastened to a flat surface. It is essential that these surfaces are perfectly flat, so that when put together they form a perfect seal (Illus 156a). Check this by holding them up to a light. Although not essential, a better casting is produced if the flattened faces are lightly rubbed on a flat charcoal block leaving a grey deposit on the cuttlefish bone which will increase its resistance to the effects of the molten metal. The object to be impressed is positioned in the centre of one half of the bone and carefully pressed in with the thumbs to almost half its depth (Illus 156b). I find that in an object such as a ring, which has most of the weight in the head, it is better to position it in the mould head downwards, so that the metal flows through the

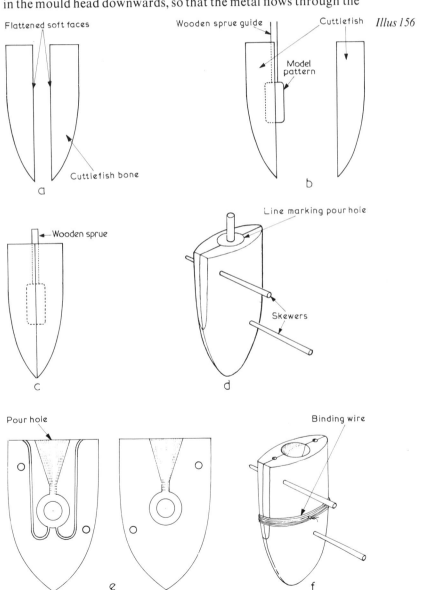

Illus 156

restricted area into the open cavity of the ring head.

Having sunk the model into the one half of the cuttlefish it is necessary to impress into this a piece of wood or metal about 3.2mm diameter and long enough to stretch from the model to the sawn off end of the cuttlefish (Illus 156b). This gives a guide as to where the pour hole, which has to be accurately positioned in this sort of split mould, should be cut. The other half of the cuttlefish is placed directly over the first half so that the squared off sawn edges line up, and the two halves pressed together. This is done by clamping them between the palms of both hands, taking care that they go together evenly and completely (Illus 156c). At this stage it is necessary to pin the two halves with a pair of tapered skewers or old needle files, forced through the bone (Illus 156). When this is done the top and one side of the cuttlefish bone should be squared off with emery paper and a circle scratched around the pour hole indicator. This should be as large in diameter as can be accommodated so that a good open mouth funnel can be formed (Illus 156d). The skewers can be pulled out and the two halves carefully split and the pattern and pour hole guide removed. The pour hole is carved into a gentle funnel shape with a sharp knife, using the impression of the pour hole guide as a centre line, and the circle scratched in the top of the mould as the diameter of the orifice. There should be no bumps or corners which might interfere with the flow of molten metal. When this has been carried out it is necessary to cut air holes in the mould so that an air lock cannot occur when the metal is poured. These simply consist of grooves scratched in with the point of a file. They are taken from the lowest points of the mould and shaped so that they come out at the top of the mould by the side of the pour hole (Illus 156e). Generally two will be enough, but for complicated shapes where there could be a number of air traps it may be necessary to have more. The air grooves should be a little deeper at the mould end but it is important that they should be fairly shallow scratches and not gouges otherwise the molten metal will run through them.

Before reassembling the mould, the model is placed back in the impression and given slight pressure to expand the indentation a little. Both halves should be free from debris before being placed together so that the flattened top and side line up. The skewers are put in place and the mould is bound with iron binding wire, and the two flattened edges checked again for alignment. The mould is then stood upright between fire bricks in readiness for the pouring (Illus 156f).

The melting and pouring of metal is very critical for if either is not carried out properly the cast will be ruined. Melting can be done in an open crucible with a large gas blow torch. It can also be done in the home-made furnace shown in Illus 166. Whatever the method the metal requires a flux and for this a very small pinch of boric acid powder is satisfactory. Too much flux will interfere with the cast. The metal is heated until it is flowing freely like water; when the surface is shiny and moving, the crucible is

Champlevé enamel and silver brooch by Stephanie Smith

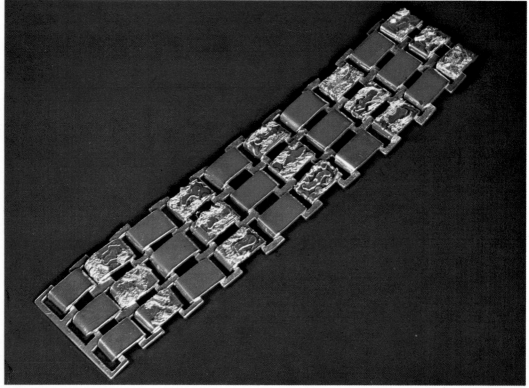

brought to the edge of the mould and the metal poured quickly and smoothly. It is essential that this operation is carried out speedily to minimise the cooling effects on the metal, and yet it must also be done smoothly in a continuous action – any hesitation or jerk will cause a break in the flow and a fault in the casting. The metal should flow through the mould into the air grooves pushing the air out before it.

Impressions can be made from any material that will withstand the force of being pressed into the cuttlefish bone. Motor car resin filling paste, wood, or lead are ideal for models. Should an object require a hole in the centre such as might be needed for setting a stone, then a piece of wood can be fitted into the hole in the model while it is forced into the cuttlefish and placed back in the mould prior to casting.

Lost Wax for the Small Workshop

Modelling may be carried out directly in wax which can be obtained in a variety of forms from the casting supplier (Illus 157). It can be modelled using a variety of dental probes and burnishers available from the dental suppliers (Illus 158). The wax, available in sheet form in a variety of thicknesses, can be cut, bent, or melted to make wax models.

Sprue

Sprue is a term given to the wax stems attached to the wax model which forms the tract through which the molten metal passes. The position of these on the model and the diameter are critical. They should be attached to the thickest part of the model and should give a smooth contoured feed into the model. Complicated shapes may require several sprues to feed the extremities and in general it is better to over sprue than to under sprue, for most casting problems may be attributed to under spruing. The diameter of the sprues should be about 3–4mm and their length between 6 and 8mm. These are attached to a main sprue stem which is about 8mm in diameter and the whole arrangement is known as a tree.

Where the metal is melted in the top of the mould over the sprue hole, the small diameter sprues on the wax model are fastened directly to the dome in the middle of the rubber mould base. The reason for this is that it is not desirable for the metal to flow into the mould before induction by whatever means you are using. The idea is that surface tension stops the molten metal from entering the sprue hole whilst melting is carried in the depression left by the rubber base. As soon as the metal is molten it is either sucked into the mould by vacuum or forced in by steam pressure. Providing you have a clear space the flask may be placed in a cradle on a length of chain with a handle and when the metal is molten this can be quickly swung round in a circle in the vertical plane so inducing the metal by centrifugal means.

When using a metal model as a pattern a 3–4mm diameter sprue

Top Silver pendant earrings with cabochon amethysts designed and made by Susan Aldcroft

Bottom Silver flexible bracelet designed and made by Elizabeth Ameghino

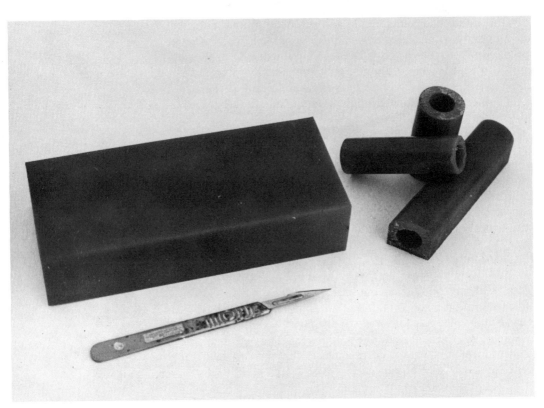

Illus 157

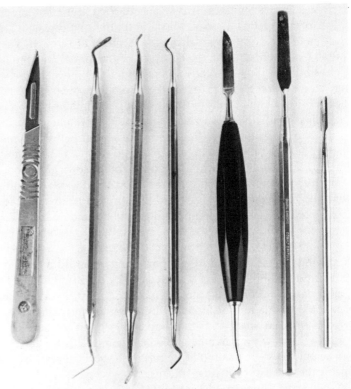

Illus 158

120

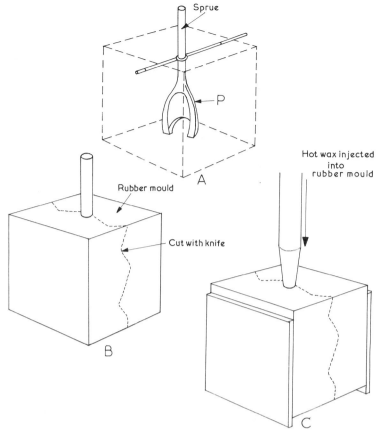

Sprue

Illus 159

P

Rubber mould

A

Cut with knife

Hot wax injected
into
rubber mould

B

C

is soldered to it (Illus 159A) and suspended in a cardboard box. This is filled with a cold cure rubber solution. Care should be taken that air pockets do not form, by using some sort of pointed stick to guide the rubber liquid round the master pattern. Having allowed the solution to set, the cardboard is peeled off and the mould sliced in half down the centre line of the model with a sharp scalpel. The blade should be worked gradually round the whole mould. Never cut straight through at one point. It is necessary to cut in and out at certain points so that a key is made and the mould may be placed back together easily and accurately (Illus 159B).

The master pattern is removed and the mould fitted together again and held firmly between two flat metal plates (Illus 159C). Some means of injecting the molten wax of a suitable type into the mould will be necessary and this can be done with a large eye dropper warmed in a flame. The wax is sucked up into this, the nozzle placed well into the sprue hole and the wax injected quickly. The mould can then be split, the wax model removed carefully and welded on to the base of the mould by melting (Illus 160).

Rubber bases are available which are shaped specially for this purpose (Illus 161). To these the wax can be fastened by melting. The wax is painted with a wetting agent available from the casting suppliers. This is allowed to dry and a section of tube, preferably stainless steel, is placed around the tree deep enough to accommodate it and about 75mm in diameter. It is sealed to the base plate with wax (Illus 162A), gummed with tape about 1in

121

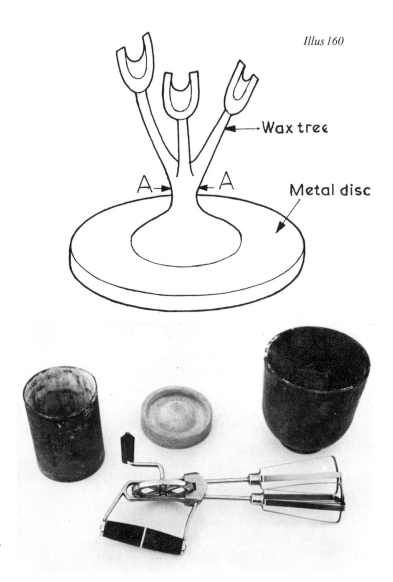

Illus 160

Wax tree

Metal disc

A ← → A

Illus 161   Casting flask, rubber base, rubber mixing bowl and hand whisk

(2.5cm) wide around the end of the tube extending it so that it can be slightly overfilled with investment, which shrinks on setting (Illus 162B). In the case of a rubber base which is a tight press fit on the tube, wax sealing is not required.

A good quality investment should be used; add it to water which should be at room temperature, mixing with a household rotary whisk for two minutes to form a smooth paste, preferably in a rubber bowl (Illus 161). (100 parts investment to 40 parts water is average.) This is poured down the side of the mould not over the wax model, while at the same time a paint brush is used to cover the wax with the investment to ensure air pockets do not occur. The mould should be overfilled and allowed to set for one hour.

The device shown in Illus 163 is fairly easily constructed or may even be bought. It relies on a close fitting pad of wet asbestos

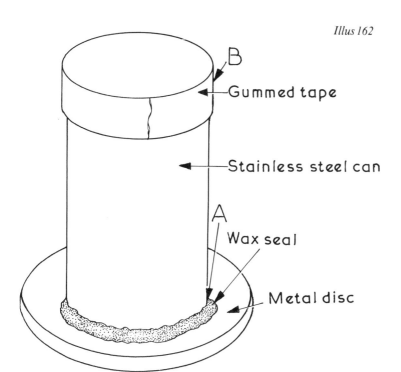

B
Gummed tape

Stainless steel can

A
Wax seal

Metal disc

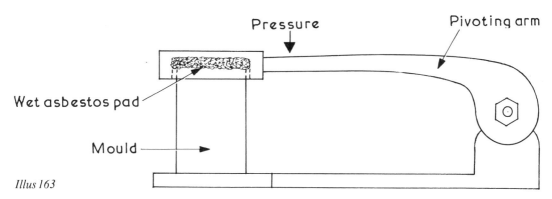

Pressure

Pivoting arm

Wet asbestos pad

Mould

Illus 163

inside a lid which is on a hinged arm so that it comes down accurately on the mould. When closed tightly on the hot mould, steam pressure is created and forces the metal into the mould.

The base to which the wax is attached is broken off and the investment protruding from the other end flattened. The mould is first gently heated at 150°C in an oven for two hours to melt the wax and then brought up to a red heat (700°C) preferably gradually over a period of four to five hours. This procedure is best carried out in a kiln, but a large gas blow torch and hearth will do, although because the procedure is accelerated to about ten minutes results cannot be guaranteed. Having brought the mould to the required temperature place it in the casting device and melt the metal and pour it into the mould and then swiftly bring down the lid with the wet asbestos, pressing it very firmly until the metal has solidified. While still hot, the mould is removed and quenched several times in a bucket of water. This causes the investment to break up releasing the castings. These are cleaned in acid pickle, and sawn off for finishing and assembly.

Vacuum Casting

Alternatively a device like that shown in Illus 164 may be obtained. It has a simple venture valve which is connected to a water tap. The water rushing through the valve causes a vacuum to build up in a chamber which has a vacuum gauge and control valves. A flat steel platform with asbestos gasket and a hole drilled through it is connected to the chamber via a control valve. When the gauge reads approximately 25in of mercury, the valve at the venture side of the chamber is closed (the other valve is obviously already in the closed position). This traps the vacuum in the chamber. The casting flask, which should have had the excess investment shaved off its blank end with a steel ruler prior to burning out in the kiln, is placed pour hole uppermost on the asbestos gasket on the steel block. The molten metal is poured into the mould and as soon as the pour hole is covered with metal the vacuum is switched on. The rapid evacuation of the investment causes the metal to fill the mould. I have found this technique to be highly successful and very suitable for the small workshop.

Another technique which relies on simple pouring without the means of forced induction is shown in Illus 165. A wax model is

Illus 164

placed on a wax stem which also has a second small diameter stem leading to the end of the model as an air hole. The procedure is the same as before, using a section of tube sealed to a base plate with wax, and filled with casting investment. But after the wax has been burned out, the molten metal is poured into the mould in exactly the same way as for cuttlefish casting. Objects of great intricacy cannot be cast by this technique nearly as successfully as with some form of forced induction.

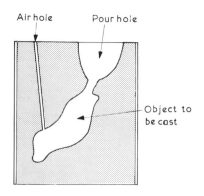

Illus 165

Gas Furnace for Melting Brass, Gold, Silver

Small gas furnaces can be bought, but a simple one can be constructed using refactory fireclay to line an iron can (Illus 166). Select a can which when lined with fireclay to a thickness of about 18–25mm has sufficient room to accommodate a melting crucible. The fireclay should be built up to a thickness of approximately 20–25mm across the bottom, sides and lid of the can. A tube 10mm in diameter should be inserted through the side of the furnace. On the lid there should be some sort of handle so that it may be easily removed. There should also be a slanting hole about 36mm in diameter at B. The gas is fed in at C and compressed air supplied from a pump, fed in at D. Both these supplies should have control taps so that a proper mixture can be achieved. The tube for the compressed air at D fits inside the tube supplying the gas. This assembly can be constructed of brass tubing silver soldered together.

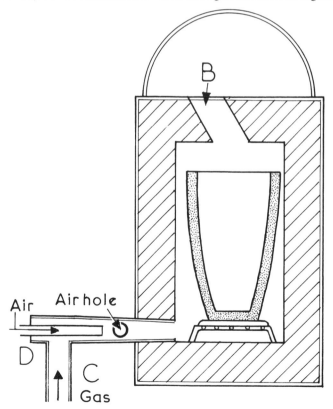

Illus 166

125

Support the crucible on some sort of stand, either made of fireclay or heavy duty iron gauze so that it stands off the base of the furnace. Place the crucible filled with small chopped pieces of metal in the furnace. Add a small pinch of boric acid powder and switch the gas on, ignite it, and place the lid on the furnace. Adjust the air to gas proportion until a flame about 36mm long is standing out of the hole at B in the lid of the furnace. Leave the crucible there until the metal's surface is running freely and has a mirror-like surface. Using a strong pair of iron tongs pick the crucible up and rock it backwards and forwards. The metal should move freely with no sign of lumps or tendencies to stick and solidify. Place back in the furnace for a couple of minutes to regain temperature lost when testing and then pour.

Casting Low Melting Point Metals

A very suitable metal for this sort of work is type metal as used in the printing industry. It has the advantage of a low melting point, pouring well and because of the addition of antimony, unlike other metals, it expands on cooling rather than contracting. This phenomenon makes the metal ideal for intricate work, and it can be copper plated as an undercoat prior to silver, gold, nickel or tin plating.

A split mould is made with investment plaster. This is most suitable for large objects which do not have undercuts and have angles sloping enough to allow the mould to be parted easily. Place the model on a tile or flat piece of glass, cover one half with clay (Illus 167) and build round the other half with investment plaster, which is allowed to set. The investment plaster half cast and the clay are removed, the investment plaster is drilled in one or two places to form a key with the other side, and well oiled all over, placed back on the model and the other half made up with investment plaster. After the investment plaster has set, separate the mould, remove the model, brush the inside of the mould with black lead, fit the two halves of the mould together and bind them. The mould can be placed in a can full of sand for support and the molten metal poured in.

Illus 167

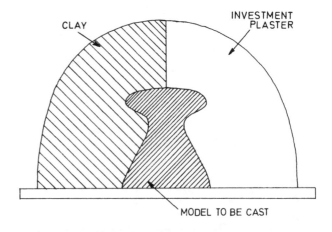

CLAY

INVESTMENT PLASTER

MODEL TO BE CAST

Lost Wax for Low Melting Point Metals

The lost wax process can be applied to this type of metal using a mixture of investment plaster mixed with water into a thick investment. Make a mould as in Illus 165 with a pour hole and air vent. In this case the wax is melted out as described on page 123 but the mould is allowed to go <u>cold</u> before casting.

A hollow casting can be produced by making a model slightly smaller than the casting required. This is done in clay without any of the fine details worked on to it. Layers of wax are built up on the model by simply immersing it in a bath of molten wax and withdrawing it until the required thickness is achieved. The fine details are worked out on the wax. The wax is scraped from the

Illus 168

Clay model

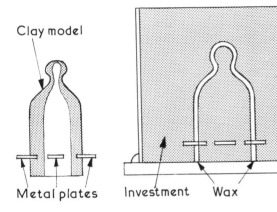

Metal plates   Investment   Wax

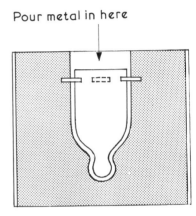

Pour metal in here

metal plates which have to support the model in the mould. Stand the model upright on its base on a board, surround it with an open ended box which is sealed to the board by tape, pour in the investment plaster. When the plaster is set, cut the base of the model back to make a pouring area for the metal, but not far enough to interfere with the metal supports. The whole thing is placed in an oven aperture downwards, to burn out and go <u>cold.</u> The mould is then placed aperture upwards and the type metal poured in. The four metal plates support the clay model when the wax is melted out so leaving the cavity for the metal. The plaster and clay are carefully broken and washed away, leaving the shell of metal which is the casting (Illus 168).

8 Electro-plating

In 1840 Elkington perfected the process of electro-deposition of both gold and silver. This was the beginning of the end for the famous traditional process called Sheffield Plate, at that time a booming industry. The Sheffield Plate process involved two thin sheets of silver sandwiching a thicker sheet of copper. The three layers were tightly clamped together and raised to a temperature not far short of the melting point of silver, at which point, with the aid of fluxes, a microscopic layer of silver and copper fused to form an alloy of lower temperature than the other metals. This phenomenon in effect soldered the sheets of metal together, in which state they were then worked. To conceal the edge of the material a distinguishing silver rim was soldered to the object on completion of forming. This was a tedious process involving a considerable amount of time in comparison with electro-plate which could be done on completion of the article with virtually no manual work other than finishing.

The principles of electro-plating are simple, if you imagine a bath of water in which two plates of metal are suspended, one being connected to the positive side of the current source and the other to the negative, these form respectively the anode and cathode. On passing an electric current through, the water splits up into its component parts causing oxygen to collect at the anode and hydrogen at the cathode. If in place of the water some solution of metal is used then the hydrogen at the cathode forms certain chemical combinations which cause the metal to separate and be deposited at the cathode. Further if a soluble anode is used of the same metal as in solution and the solution is of a suitable nature, then as fast as metal is deposited at the cathode so it is replaced by dissolution of the anode.

A simple plating plant can be constructed using a battery charger, with a means of controlling the current wired into the circuit. The simplest method is to wire a domestic light socket into the positive side of the wiring and by fitting bulbs of various wattages the current can be controlled. The lower the wattage the lower the current. You will have to learn by trial whether you require a 15, 40, or 60 watt bulb (Illus 169). If you are fortunate enough to be able to afford the proper equipment it will contain a variable rheostat, volt meter and ammeter. Although a volt meter is useful for controlling a bath, if all is normal, it is the current density read as amps on the ammeter which is critical and from which the rate of deposition is controlled. By comparing amps with the time in solution the depth of a deposit can be calculated.

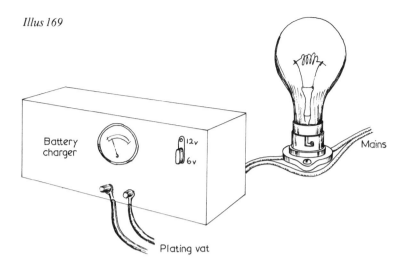

Illus 169

Battery charger

12v

6v

Mains

Plating vat

Electro-Cleaning

Cathodic cleaning is simple to do using the plating equipment with a solution of caustic soda (approximately ½lb–1gal) maintained at a temperature of 60°C on a gas or electric ring and thermometer. The object to be cleaned is attached to the negative side and a sheet iron anode connected to the positive side. The object is immersed for about a minute at about 5 volts or sufficient current to cause bubbles to stream from it, and then removed and immediately immersed in a rinse from which it is then taken to the plating vat.

Degreasing and Plating

The object to be plated is cleaned by degreasing in either a hot caustic solution (approximately ½lb–1gal) or in a detergent solution. It is essential that all grease is removed from the surfaces but do not use soap as it leaves a deposit which will interfere and spoil the process. Should there be any problems such as peeling or bubbling of the deposited metal then the first thing to investigate is the efficiency of the degreasing stage.

The object is then immersed in the plating solution by suspending from a bar across the bath connected to the negative side of the current source (Illus 170). It is important that immersion takes place after the current is switched on; never immerse in the solution prior to switching on. It is always better to start with a low current, gradually increasing it until the required deposition rate and colour is achieved.

Gilding

It is preferable to buy the prepared salts which are simply added to distilled water to form the required solution. Care should be taken for gilding solutions contain a high proportion of cyanide and whilst it might be expected that a person would not unwittingly drink the solution directly out of the beaker, great care should be

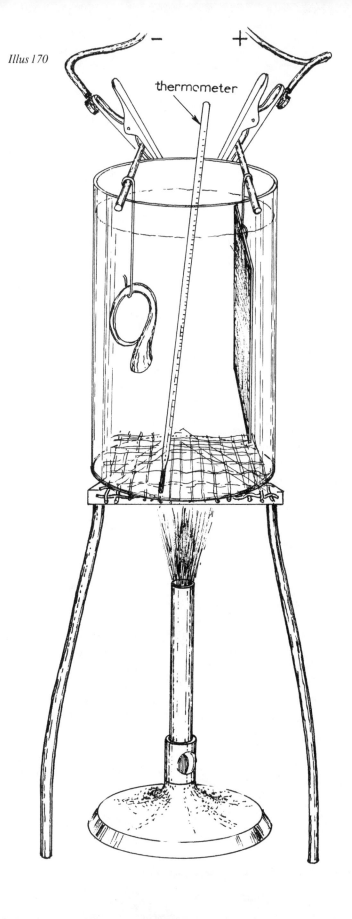

Illus 170

thermometer

exercised should the solution splash onto any surface or hands and face. Mop spillage up quickly, use rubber gloves and swill away with plenty of water to dilute.

The gilding solution should be maintained at a temperature of approximately 60°C in a pyrex beaker on a gas ring and a thermometer. Below this temperature a pale deposit is given and above this a darker deposit. If a number of items are being treated it is essential that the solution is maintained at a constant temperature to give consistent colour. In this solution suspend an anode (a sheet of stainless steel) which is connected to the positive side of the current source. A bar is placed across the beaker and this is connected to the cathode or negative side of the current. The current is switched on and the jewellery piece suspended from the bar by a length of copper wire. Deposition will start and the object should be checked from time to time until correct colour and thickness is acquired.

Silver Plating

Silver plating differs from gilding in that it is essential to have what is termed a Striking solution to deposit the initial foundation or keying layer of silver on which subsequent heavier deposits are laid. The strike consists of a plating solution of high cyanide and low metallic content which is operated at a high current. The contents of the solution should be approximately 0.1 per cent silver, 10 per cent cyanide, and the object lowered into it with the current on, left there for a few seconds, removed and immediately immersed in the plating solution proper. The current passing through the object whilst in the strike should be approximately ten times that used in the plating solution, which should be run at about 1 volt with a current density of 10amps/sq ft. The strike can be made by adding a little of the plating salts to a vat of distilled water and then dissolving in some cyanide. Again it must be emphasised that these solutions are highly poisonous and care should be taken that casual handling does not occur.

Silver plating salts are bought ready to dissolve in distilled water which should be used for all plating solutions. There are other techniques of depositing precious metals involving the processes of amalgamation with mercury, but they are not to be recommended for while the results are excellent, the danger to health from just handling mercury, which can be absorbed by the skin, makes its use very risky.

Nickel Plating

The solution consists simply of double salts of nickel and ammonia in the quantities of $\frac{3}{4}$lb to 1 gallon of distilled water. The water should be hot to aid dissolution and the solution filtered through a calico filter into the vat. Ready-made plating solutions are available and generally give better results than a home brew for they include many additives in the form of levellers and brighteners. The procedure is the same as for other deposits using suitable nickel anodes which need to have a large surface area and be placed inside nylon bags, eg old stockings. Surfaces that have previously been nickelled should have all traces of the old deposit removed (see Stripping).

Copper Plating

This process may be carried out either non-electrically or electrically. The first process gives a superficial coating such as is required for oxidising or bronzing whilst the second produces a thicker heavy deposit. The immersion process requires a solution of 1½ pints of water and 8oz of copper sulphate and another solution of 6 pints of water to 2 pints of hydrochloric acid. The latter solution should then have about half a cupful of the first solution added to it giving a solution suitable for deposition. As the action of the solution diminishes so a little of the first solution is used to replenish. It is necessary to strike the surface of the object being plated by firstly immersing until the surface is coated with the reddish deposit, then scratch brushing this until bright, and re-immersing when quite a good deposit may be achieved.

For electro-deposition dissolve 10oz of copper chloride in 2 pints of distilled water than add liquid ammonia in small quantities during which a green deposit (precipitate) will form on the bottom, but keep adding ammonia until this re-dissolves and the solution is blue when 3 pints of distilled water must be added. Prepare another solution of 1¼lb of potassium cyanide in 5 pints of water, add this gradually to the first solution and allow it all to stand for a day before filtering into a vat. During plating the solution should be maintained at approximately 60°C.

Stripping

Prior to replating it is necessary to strip off existing deposits. The following solutions will be required:

Gold may be stripped by a reversal of the plating operation or with a solution of 1 part nitric acid to 4 parts hydrochloric and simple immersion but care has to be exercised for the acid is very active and should be diluted 1 part acid to 4 parts water.

Silver can be dissolved in a solution of 1 part nitric acid to 8 parts sulphuric acid by immersion. Frequent inspection is necessary to ensure that all is well and the acid solution diluted 1 part acid to 4 parts water.

Nickel is stripped in a solution of 20 parts sulphuric acid to 5 parts water, to which is added 5 parts nitric acid. Immerse the object to be stripped and watch it carefully until the old deposit is removed.

Gilding Treatments

An etched surface can be put on cast brass to give a frosted finish which is very attractive after gilding (sometimes called matt dip). The solution consists of equal parts nitric acid and sulphuric acid to each pint of which is added half a teaspoonful of salt. The article is dipped in this momentarily, removed and immediately immersed in a cold water swill.

A gilt surface can be treated to give an effect called ormolu. Using equal parts oxide of iron powder, alum, and saltpetre, make a paste with annatto. Coat the surfaces with the paste, leaving for a short time and swill in a solution containing the same constituents. The surface may be treated again until the required effect is achieved. Should anything go wrong then the treated surface is dipped in the sulphuric acid pickle to bring back to normal.

Gold Colouring

Gold may be treated in a solution consisting of ½oz of common salt and alum and 2oz of saltpetre dissolved in a little hot water. Heat the solution in a pyrex beaker until it just simmers and dip the article in for a few minutes, withdraw, and swill in cold water. Repeat this several times until the required colour is achieved.

Metal Colouring

An important part of any metal object is the finish imparted to the surface. It is all very well producing pleasant shapes and forms but these can be entirely ruined by poor finishing and a lack of consideration of the colouring of metals. There are various solutions and techniques to suit the various metals in use by the jeweller. Unfortunately most of the chemicals used are highly poisonous and therefore great care should be exercised. A well ventilated room with a lockable cupboard is essential and a worktop covered with acid resistant PVC or formica will also be needed.

When working in base metals such as brass, copper and nickel, the usual thing to do is to either gold or silver plate the surface but this is not always necessary for these metals can be treated in their own right to produce an amazing range of colours and effects. Brass can be so treated that any of the following finishes may be given to it: black, verde, antique, green, gun-metal and any of the finishes that can be applied to copper can be given by heavy copper plating of the brass.

Black Nickelling (On Brass)

A black surface of great intensity capable of receiving a high polish and able to withstand oxidation to a remarkable degree is simply carried out using the electro-plating equipment, and once applied adheres most tenaciously and can be treated as an ordinary nickelled surface.

The chemicals and the order they are dissolved are as follows. Dissolve 12oz of double salt of nickel and ammonia in 1 gallon of water, add to this 3oz of sulphocyanide of potash and 2oz of carbonate of copper. Make a second solution by taking 2oz of white arsenic in powdered form and dissolve in sufficient carbonate of ammonia and a little water to make a solution. A little warmth will probably be needed to dissolve the ingredients of both solutions. Although I have said heat the solutions to dissolve the chemicals, ensure this is carried out very gently and on no account should they be boiled. The arsenic solution should be clear and can now be added to the first solution.

As for any plating process it is essential that the article to be plated is completely grease-free and the surface free from unwanted defects as these will show up more prominently under the black surface. The anodes for black plating are exactly the same as those for white nickel plating. The blackness of the finish is governed by the quantity of arsenic and it will require a few tests by the operator to ensure things are working properly. The finish should be an intense velvety black. Should this not be the case then more of the arsenic solution should be added a little at a time until consistent results are obtained. Always remember it is easier to add solution than to remove it.

This finish can be applied to iron, steel, copper, German silver and silver. All nickel deposits, but in particular the black finish, require the anodes to be kept scrupulously clean so frequent scraping of these is necessary.

Gun-Metal Finish

Iron in the form of fine wire is dissolved in commercial hydrochloric acid to form a saturated solution. The iron wire should be placed in a pyrex beaker, covered with the acid. Then add half as much water as acid and warm to hasten the action. On cooling a certain amount of iron should precipitate out as green-coloured crystals, indicating that the solution is a saturated one. Add to every quart of this solution ½oz of white arsenic in a powdered form and gently warm as well as stir to assist the dissolving of the arsenic. You must not overheat the solution as the arsenic will volatilise and be lost. If on cooling crystals begin to form then add a little more water to re-dissolve. Filter the solution through cotton wool or a paper handkerchief placed in a funnel, and the colour of the solution should be a clear transparent dark green.

The object should be given a fine matt finish preferably by sand blasting which certain specialists can do for you, but scratch brushing is quite satisfactory. The surface must not be handled or in any way be allowed to become greasy. The deposit is put on in the plating machine by using carbon or nickel anodes and passing about 6 volts through the article. If you use a nickel anode you will need to add a small quantity of nickel chloride to the solution. However, the result of using a nickel anode is to give a hard, more wear-resistant surface. It is important that the current is switched on before the article is lowered into the solution in order that an even coating is achieved. A light coating can be achieved in a few seconds and is suitable if the highlights are to be relieved. A few minutes are normally required to build up a reasonable coating. After immersion swill well in warm water and scratch brush till the required shade is achieved, after which is must be lacquered.

A variety of chains

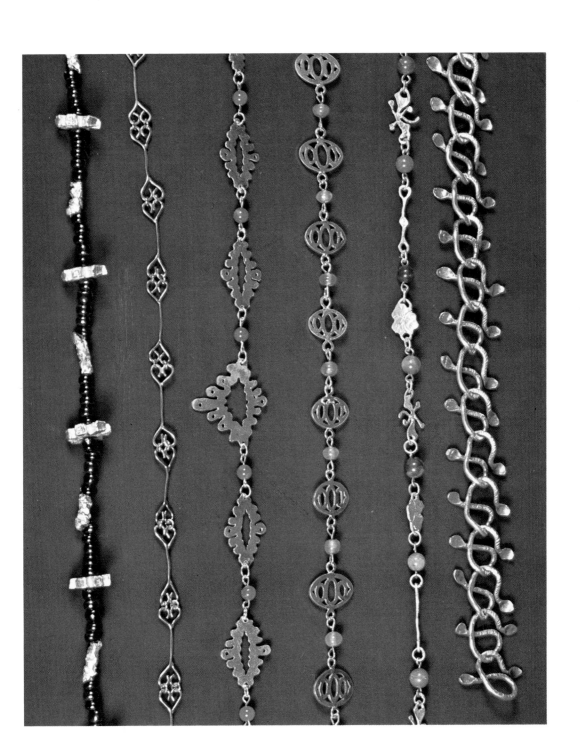

Crystallising the Surface of Cast Brass

This process is really only effective on cast brass where the crystal structure is unaffected by rolling and manipulation. The main consideration is the type of brass used which should be of such a type as to have by nature a large grain structure. Common yellow mixture is quite suitable and should be poured at a good high temperature. The lower the temperature the smaller the grain structure and the poorer the effect of crystallisation.

The solution consists of $\frac{1}{4}$ gallon concentrated hydrochloric acid, 8oz of bichromate of potash crystals and 1 gallon of water. Firstly the bichromate of potash is dissolved in the water which should be warm and then the acid is added. You can use the solution hot or cold with the same results but it takes about thirty minutes to achieve with the cold solution. After this it is essential that the surface is not handled and that it is lacquered immediately.

Black Brass

A black finish can be imparted to brass by making a solution of silver nitrate and copper nitrate in equal quantities in water, forming a strong saturated solution. The article should be cleaned and grease-free as for all these processes, when it can be dipped into the solution, drawn out and gently warmed over a flame until evaporation is complete. The article is then swilled and dried.

Colouring Copper

There are a number of finishes which can be applied to copper and in turn all of these finishes can be applied to other metals if they are copper plated. Many of the processes applicable to brass can also be applied to copper and likewise many of the processes can be applied to other alloys of copper such as gilding metal.

Royal Copper

The first process to be considered gives the metal a deep cherry red of excellent lustre having the appearance of enamel. It also is a very durable finish. It simply involves buying saltpetre in crystal form and melting it in an iron pot over a bunsen. Take care not to overheat as instead of the red oxide you will get a black oxide which occurs at about the boiling point of the chemical. The exact temperature is 593°C and to determine the working temperature try a few test pieces which should remain immersed for a few seconds until oxidation is completed. On removal these should be immersed and allowed to cool in a bath of high flash point oil which prevents staining of the article. On removal the object is wiped dry, gently buffed and finally coated with a clear lacquer.

Green Copper

Green surface corrosion similar to that which occurs on copper naturally after many years in the atmosphere can be achieved by

(*Top*)   Silver and pavé-set fish brooch designed and made by Sandra Thomas

(*Bottom*)   Forged 9ct gold bracelet designed and made by Hamish Bowie

137

actually creating an atmosphere artificially. Great care is needed to be sure of consistent results. Mix 2oz of hydrochloric acid and 2oz of acetic acid in 100oz of water and damp a quantity of sawdust with this solution. Do not over-wet, just dampness is required, and add a little ground chalk or limestone into the sawdust to improve the action and finished result. Clean and degrease the surface to be treated and place it in the sawdust. Leave this overnight by when the object should be covered with green sediment. Dry carefully and finish with a scratch brush if necessary, after which lacquer with a clear lacquer.

Another method used to produce this finish is a simple dipping solution consisting of $\frac{1}{2}$oz sal ammoniac, 1oz hydrochloric acid, 20oz acetic acid and 2oz of copper nitrate, and dissolving these use the solution hot. Immerse the copper for a few moments, withdraw and without rinsing remove, allow to dry, and fix with a clear lacquer.

Oxidising

The best method of oxidising copper is by means of a solution of hydrosulphide of ammonia. To achieve good results it is essential that care is taken in the preparation of the metal which should be completely free from grease. The potassium sulphide should be diluted in the proportions of 4oz to 1 gallon of water and should be used cold as the deposit is more adherent than that achieved by a hot solution. The solution has a very limited shelf life so frequent testing is necessary prior to use to ensure all is well. Swill the oxidised item in water and if required the highlights can be relieved with a scratch brush or polishing mop.

Colouring Silver
Oxidising

As with copper use a solution of hydrosulphide of ammonia although a weaker solution is required for silver of the order of 4oz of hydrosulphide of ammonia to 1 gallon of water. The procedure is exactly as that for copper but in the case of silver plated items ensure that there is a heavy deposit of silver and that the dip is a short one as the sulphur will unite with the silver. If the plating deposit is thin then one solution to the oxidation problem is to deposit a fine copper layer using the plating vat. This must be very light, just the merest blush of copper is required. The job can then be dipped in the solution for just sufficient time to produce the oxide required without affecting the silver plate. The highlights can be relieved using polishing techniques or a scratch brush.

9 Plastics

The chief advantages of plastics are their ease of application to mass production, forming, low cost, fantastic range of colours, numerous degrees of transparency and opalescence. All of these characteristics can be used and applied in many different ways, but one factor must be borne in mind and that is cost of production. Because of low material cost plastics have a very definite advantage over many other materials for production of simple, fashionable, inexpensive jewellery. This advantage should not be lost in complicated design and production methods.

There is a great deal of room for development in the design of jewellery containers and plastic is a very fine material for their production (Illus 171). But whatever is designed one must bear in mind that plastics constitute an important part of the modern environment, which affects anything connected with it whether it be clothes, jewellery or any of the ancillary articles. I feel that to produce an object which is aesthetically in keeping, one must consider those things which make up that environment. Plastics are used in architecture, industrial design, interior design, and in numerous other ways, and in keeping with this plastic jewellery designs must be of equal quality. Although a great deal of inexpensive jewellery

Illus 171   Acrylic ring boxes designed and made by Hamish Bowie

is produced in plastic, a lot of it is poorly thought out and does not make full advantage of the material. It is often used to make nothing more than a cheap copy of similarly stereotyped metal jewellery. This should not be so, for plastic is a material in its own right and should be treated as such with no inhibitions about the way it should or should not be used.

The term plastic, if defined, is the state of plasticity of a material or the state in which it can be moulded or shaped. Clay, wax, and plaster are plastic substances, so the term can by no means be restricted to those materials of the very latest origin. Even the most primitive of men have used mud for building huts and this composition of earth and water must have been the earliest plastic material to have been used by man.

It is interesting to learn that nature provides its own plastics. Shellac, produced by the Lac fly, and bitumen, which was used by the Egyptians, are examples. Our own bodies are made up from high polymers which scientists are constantly trying to reproduce. The whole field of plastics is fascinating although the development of man made plastics has only taken place within the past hundred years. Of the new manufactured materials which are commonly termed plastics, there are two basic types, thermoplastics and thermosetting plastics. The first type can be repeatedly softened by heating and then hardens on cooling, eg acrylic. The second is first softened by heat, moulded, and hardened under heat by chemical reaction. Their composition is altered by the reaction and they cannot be softened again. Because of the ease with which thermoplastics are manipulated they are ideal as a material for the production of inexpensive, colourful, fashionable jewellery; also for jewellery boxes suitable for both display and functional purposes.

Cellulosic Plastics

Celluloid was the first thermoplastic produced in Britain under the name of Parksine, by Alexander Parkes. However, it was not successful until the Hyatt brothers of America developed the process and began manufacture. All attempts to render it non-inflammable were unsuccessful; but non-inflammable cellulose acetate was developed which has similar mechanical properties to celluloid. It came into prominence during World War I when it was made into a solution with acetone to form a non-inflammable 'dope' for the canvas coverings of aeroplanes. As the market for this collapsed after the war a new type of silk called rayon was developed from it by extruding a thick solution of acetate in acetone into warm air through tiny holes in a steel die called a spinneret. Later acetate was used as a moulding material and with the advent of the injection moulding machine became the first material to be used in this way. There are many varieties of cellulosic plastics now available. Their properties vary but this enables the jewellery maker to choose the right type to suit a particular application.

Cellulose Acetate

Available in a wide range of transparent colours the material calls for new design methods. Direct use of the material to produce a design and prototype is simple; for shaping can be carried out easily with simple hand tools such as scissors, leather working tools, and some jewellery making tools. The sheet can be heated in an electric oven set at between 150°C and 170°C. If your enamelling kiln has a fine control down to this temperature then it can be used. Alternatively boiling water will do. Gas ovens are not really suitable. When at the correct temperature the sheet will be pliable enough to shape over simple formers (Illus 172). These may be made from plaster or wood. Some jewellery implements can be used, ie the doming block and punch. A disc of acetate when heated may be pressed into one of the depressions and held there under pressure with the appropriate punch until the plastic cools and hardens. The process of curving in one direction as described in Chapter 1 may be applied to plastics. The only difference is that the plastic has to be held in the forming tool until it cools and stiffens.

Acrylic

Acrylic is the trade name for polymethyl methacrylate which comes under the group name of acrylic plastics. In the 1870s various acrylic compounds were known to chemists, who found that when trying to purify them by distillation some compounds set into a transparent elastic mass and others into white solids. In 1913 a German chemist suggested that some of these compounds could be developed into substitutes for rubber but no progress was made because of the lack of any method of producing the compound industrially.

It was not until the 1930s that acrylics and many other new polymers such as polythene, nylon, neoprene, polystyrene, and polyvinyl chloride, were developed as materials for industry. Acrylic is obtained in sheet form, as rod or tubes, and also in a special granular form for injection moulding. One of its outstanding properties is its transparency. Because of this camera lenses

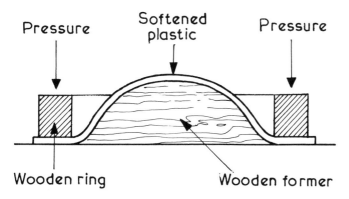

Illus 172

made from it are efficient but are not so resistant to abrasion as glass. Most contact lenses are now made from acrylic instead of glass and more comfortable. Acrylic lends itself to the phenomenon of the 'piping of light'. A beam of light can be transmitted through a considerable length of acrylic rod, commonly termed fibre optics.

A great deal of shaping of perspex can be carried out with simple wooden formers manipulating the plastic in hot water.

Certain techniques can be used on perspex and other acrylics. The forming temperature and techniques of manipulation for perspex and acetate sheet are the same. On heating over a wide temperature range perspex is gradually transformed from its hard state to rubberiness. At about 85°C visible signs of demoulding appear – a phenomenon caused by a property of the material to tend to return to the form it was originally manufactured in. At 120°C it will become pliable but the ideal temperature for shaping is between 150 and 170°C and this is achieved in an oven. From the oven the heated material is brought to the mould and ideally kept at 120–150°C during the actual shaping operation. The air pressures required by perspex are relatively low, being in the region of not more than 40lb per square inch. With this it may be free blown (Illus 173) or blown into a mould (Illus 174). In fact manipulation using simple wooden formers applied with hand pressure is quite sufficient for a great deal of work (Illus 172).

Acrylic is an ideal medium for shaping by machine or hand using either wood or metal working equipment (Illus 175). It is es-

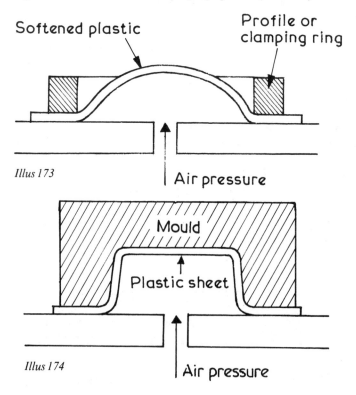

Softened plastic

Profile or clamping ring

Illus 173

Air pressure

Mould

Plastic sheet

Illus 174

Air pressure

sential that tools are always kept well sharpened to avoid local heating of the material due to excessive friction. With a slight modification ordinary twist drills are suitable for perspex. The drills are adapted by blunting the cutting faces with a grind stone. The effect is to square the edges so that the drill scrapes its way through rather than cuts (Illus 176). Circular saws are preferable to band saws for straight cuts and strips. Fret saws, dental burrs and engraving tools may be used for cutting and modelling. Illus 175 shows a pair of rings cut from sheet acrylic, designed and made by Elizabeth Ameghino. Band saws, particularly the large type, are suitable for intricate shapes which circular saws will not do, because the length of the blade readily dissipates heat.

Illus 176

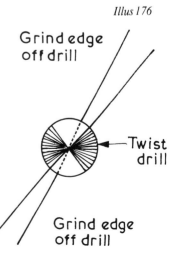

Grind edge off drill

Twist drill

Grind edge off drill

Glueing Plastics

There are definite techniques to make a more satisfactory job of glueing a piece of work together. The problem is to exclude air bubbles from forming in the glue as the two surfaces are brought together. The idea is to use plenty of glue and hinge the two pieces with cellotape so that they can be brought together slowly in such a manner that air is not trapped but pushed out by the action (Illus 177). Dropping one surface directly on the other will cause air to be trapped and bubbles to be formed. Chloroform administered from a hypodermic syringe may be used as glue. It melts the sur-

143

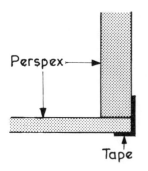 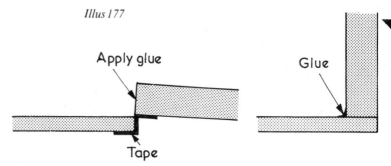

face and the two pieces are brought together in the same manner before the chloroform evaporates.

Finishing

Thermoplastics can be quite simply finished using a succession of finer grades of emery paper, sandpaper or wet and dry paper which is an emery paper that can be used with water lubricant. It can then be polished on calico buffs using the normal wax dressing such as white rouge. The technique is to keep a balance between pressure applied and speed of the mop to avoid overheating. Vapour polishing of intricate parts can be done with trichlorethelene but this is definitely too dangerous and complex for the amateur. Flame polishing of edges can be carried out using a very hot clean flame such as is produced by oxygen and hydrogen. The surface is touched momentarily with the hottest part of the flame so as to glaze it but not to burn it. For good results it is essential that the surface is well prepared with the finest wet and dry paper.

Polyester Resin

There are many plastics in use for decorating and colouring jewellery. The most significant of these are polyester resins. Sold under a variety of trade names they are supplied as a transparent syrupy fluid to which a hardener is added. This triggers a chemical reaction during which the temperature of the resin rises. It becomes gelatinous and then hardens to a firm, transparent mass.

Whilst in the liquid state special colouring pigments, available in a wide range of colours may be added when the hardener has been thoroughly mixed with the resin. To obtain a transparent effect only the smallest quantity of pigment should be added. A drop gathered on the end of a match stick to begin with; adding more will intensify the colour until it eventually becomes opaque. It is important to stir well to produce even colouration.

The resin may be used in place of enamel in metal jewellery and many of the constructions made for enamel will suit resin (Illus 178). Objects may be encapsulated in the transparent resin. For this special moulds are available from most craft shops or you may make your own. Polythene, polypropylene and hard PVC are all suitable materials for moulds. Many household containers are made from these materials. Bowls and ice cube containers are often made from polythene, which can be identified as a pliable

milky looking substance with a waxy surface which makes the removal of the casting easy.

It is difficult for the layman to identify the various plastics. Polystyrene, a transparent brittle material in which food and sundry small items are packed is not suitable and will dissolve. It is important therefore to carry out the following test: a spot of resin is placed on the plastic, clean it off with a rag after ten minutes and if the surface is rough and sticky then the container will not be suitable for resin casting. Glass and wood are suitable materials for moulds but require treatment with a special release wax obtainable from craft shops, particularly wood. Ordinary furniture wax polish will make a suitable release agent but it must be non-silicone.

Tin lids and sections of metal tubing glued to a glass base, treated with release wax make suitable moulds. Circular moulds

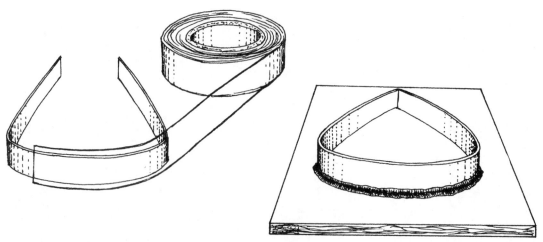

Illus 179 A strip of metal
approximately 0.25mm thick,
very thin but not as thin as foil,
is bent to shape and then bound
with cellophane adhesive tape.
The excess tape is trimmed back
to the metal with scissors. This
is placed on a sheet of glass and
sealed to it with modelling clay.
The resin can then be poured in
as required

can be made from metal or glass discs. Masking or similar adhesive tape may be wrapped round the edge as in Illus 179 to form a
wall.

Having selected a mould and decided on the object to be
embedded some resin is mixed with the appropriate amount of
hardener, usually about 2 per cent. The mould is half filled with
resin and allowed to stand for two hours during which time it will
react, increasing in temperature and the surface becoming gelatinous. At this point the object or objects to be embedded are placed
in the resin (Illus 180). Delicate things like flowers may be placed
sooner when the resin is still liquid to reduce the risk of bubbles
forming beneath them. The resin is allowed to harden. When the
first layer of resin is hard and cold, indicating the reaction is complete, the second layer is mixed and slowly poured into the mould
so that air is not trapped. This is allowed to harden overnight. The
surface of the resin will be tacky due to the oxidation which hap-

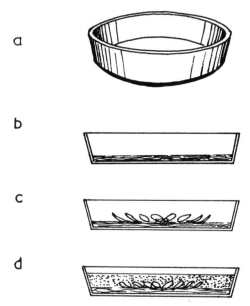

Illus 180   a the mould is
rubbed with release wax; the
mould can be made from sheet
metal, or glazed ceramic or
polythene moulds can be
bought; b the first layer of resin
is poured in – coloured if a
coloured background is
required; wait until the surface
is gelatinous which takes about
2 hours; c the objects to be
embedded are placed on this
layer to which they will stick;
allow this first layer to harden;
d the second layer is poured on
after the first layer is set. This,
the last layer, is allowed to set
and the casting removed from
the mould and polished

pens during the hardening process. When the mould is removed this has to be polished.

Polishing the surface of resin is much the same as for acrylics. It has firstly to be cut back to a smooth regular surface with emery or sand paper, preferably wet and dry paper which is a waterproof type used extensively in the motor car industry and is available from most motor accessory shops. It is lubricated with water which prevents clogging and reduces the risk of overheating the surface of the resin by friction; it also removes the sticky layer very quickly. Stretch and fasten the emery paper to a flat board using drawing pins, or adhesive tape. Work from the coarse grade of emery paper (grade 3) through to a fine grade (grade 00). Work the resin until a fine, smooth even matt surface is achieved. This surface can then be polished using a specially prepared polishing

Illus 181

paste which is applied to a soft cloth pinned to a board. The casting is rubbed on the material under pressure until a polished surface is achieved.

You may experiment with colouring the layers of resin. For instance the first background layer could be opaque colour whilst the top layer remains transparent, white, or slightly tinted.

Dried flowers, grasses, dry thistle heads, fir cones, shells, household items like pins, paper clips, beads, or pieces of coloured glass may be embedded in attractive arrangements. The limiting factor is that objects containing moisture may not be embedded, and therefore flowers have to be dried. This process can be accelerated by pressing the flowers under blotting paper with an iron until they are dry. Illus 181 shows small units with shells embedded. These may be drilled at a point on the perimeter and a jewellery fitting glued in to take a chain. These and a range of other types of fittings are available from craft shops.

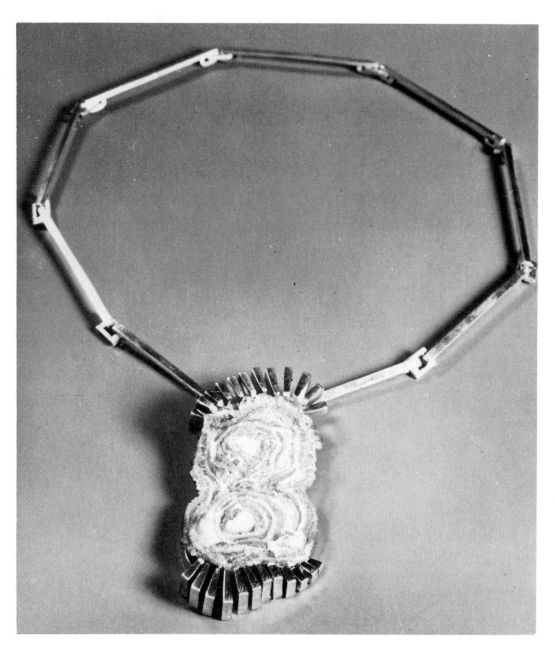

Illus 182   Grey crystalline
quartz and silver pendant and
silver chain designed and made
by Hamish Bowie

Appendix 1

Gold

Gold, silver and platinum are termed the Noble Metals, and based on their value is the economy of our own, and nearly every other human civilization.

Gold almost certainly was the first metal to have been used by man. Largely because of its bright yellow appearance, primitive man gathered grains and large lumps which he found in river beds, and tied them together with thong and horsehair to form the first gold jewellery. The Goldsmith's craft developed into the decoration of flint knives as more was learned about the qualities of this metal.

From these early beginnings came a pinnacle of craftsmanship in gold which has never been surpassed when the gorgeous gold spiral shells of the first Egyptian Dynasty 5500 BC and the chains and gilded work of Cleopatra and the Romans were produced. The remarkable developments are all due to the properties of the metal, which not only has a unique colour, but is tarnish resistant and amazingly ductile. A measure of this ductility can be shown when 300,000 sheets of pure gold can be laid one on top of the other. The depth will not exceed 25mm.

Gold is found in most parts of the world and with the exception of aluminium and iron is more generally distributed than any other metal but in very small proportions. It is rarely found in sufficient quantity to make mining a practical proposition. Where such quantities have been found it has meant toil, greed, wealth, and often death to man who finds gold so desirable. Some of the purest native gold has been found in Australian and Russian mines. But it is rarely found as a pure material and is generally alloyed with copper, silver, or occasionally palladium, rhodium, and other metals. The greatest area for gold mining is South Africa and at the turn of the century 80 per cent of the total world gold yield came from within a twelve mile radius of Johannesburg. Most of the gold is taken from quartz rock using deep bore mining, similar to coal mining. But dredging and panning still continue.

Gold is soluble in cyanide solution and this is often used to separate the metal. Mercury is also used because of its ability to form an amalgam with gold. This amalgamation process is immediate and mercury will contain up to 13 per cent of gold when it changes from a liquid to a paste. This phencmenon has caused many jewellers quite a problem, as immediately a gold item is exposed to mercury the amalgam forms on the surface of the gold so making it white. People involved in laboratory work are susceptible to this and many a jeweller has been accused of supplying a ring which was not gold. However, a simple buffing process removes the amalgam and restores the colour. Pure gold melts at a temperature of 1061°C; the carat alloys all melt below this.

The metal is readily beaten into forms but because of its softness is not durable. To prevent it from wearing away it is alloyed with various other metals, usually copper and silver in proportions balanced to give the required colour. A higher copper content will produce red gold which tends to be brittle, or a higher silver content produces a pale or green gold which tends to be soft. When it is alloyed with nickel white gold is produced. In order that the quality of gold may be determined a system called 'Hall Marking' was instituted in Britain in 1327 through a charter given to the Worshipful Company of Goldsmiths by Edward I. The first quality of hall markable gold alloy was 19 carats determined by calling pure gold 24 carats and fusing 19 parts gold with 5 parts alloy. The range of qualities was extended and today the standard qualities are 22ct, 18ct, 14ct and 9ct, the last three in both yellow and white gold. For all of these alloys there is a suitable solder available in three melting points so when ordering solder state the carat gold being worked on and the melting point of the solder which can be simply termed hard, medium or easy.

Silver

Silver has pure white colour and presents a perfect metallic lustre which is one of its greatest features. With the exception of gold it is the most malleable and ductile of all metals; one gramme may be drawn into a wire 300ft long and be beaten into a sheet 0.00025mm thick, transmitting a blue light. It also occurs in minute quantities in sea water. It is widely distributed over the earth's surface and is found as an amalgam with mercury, and as an alloy with platinum, gold, copper and other metals and large masses have been found weighing several hundred pounds in its native cubic crystal form. It is the best known conductor of heat and electricity, and so is used in the production of electrical components for aircraft and in similar special fields.

The pure metal is used for an enamelling surface where the presence of copper is not desired. For other applications Sterling quality is used (92.5 per cent silver) and to a lesser extent Britannia quality (95.84 per cent). On the hall mark Sterling silver is denoted by the Lion Passant and Britannia by the figure of Britannia. The melting point of pure silver is 961°C, the alloys somewhat lower.

Several solders of different melting points are available including a special high melting point enamelling solder for use on articles which have to be enamelled after soldering. It should be used with care as it melts only shortly before the silver.

Platinum

Platinum is the next most ductile and malleable metal known. It is exceedingly rare, mostly found alloyed to one or more of the rare metals such as ruthenium, palladium, rhodium, iridium, or osmium. With a melting point of 1775°C it is only exceeded in fusibility by two or three of the even rarer metals. It resists oxidation at any temperature and is not affected by nitric, hydrochloric or sulphuric acids in the cold, but is soluble in hot aqua regia. The colour is tin white or steel grey with a metallic lustre used to a great extent these days for setting diamonds. Solders range in melting point from 950°C to 1200°C and to 1400°C. The latter is melted with oxy-hydrogen or acetylene and goggles must be worn to avoid eye damage which can be caused by the intense white heat.

Palladium

This steel grey metal resembling platinum, is the most fusible of the platinum group with a melting point of 1500°C. It is malleable and ductile but approaches steel in hardness and, like platinum, has a great resistance to corrosion. It is occasionally seen in jewellery but is not in general use.

Rhodium

Used in the jewellery industry to a great extent in electro-plating processes to give a brilliant tarnish resistant finish, particularly on white gold which is never truly white. Its melting point is 2000°C and, when pure, it is insoluble in acids or aqua regia. Hard, ductile and malleable at red heat, it is white with a bluish tinge resembling polish aluminium.

Copper

It is a peculiar red colour and will take on a very fine polish. It is extremely ductile and malleable. Melting at 1050°C it is a good conductor of heat and electricity. It is readily soldered with silver solders and may be annealed in the normal way, although if required, when quenched in cold water it softens more than if allowed to cool naturally. It can be deposited on other metals either with or without electricity and is important as a foundation for most electro deposits. The ability to form alloys readily makes it very useful and it is the basis of pinchbeck, gilding metal, brass and bronze.

Gilding Metal

An alloy of copper and zinc in the percentages 80–20 it is very suitable for the production of hollow ware and jewellery which is to be plated. It is ductile and malleable but not as hard as brass and has a melting point lower than copper.

Pewter

Pewter is an alloy of four parts tin to one part lead which melts at a much lower temperature (approximately 275°C) than lead. It can be easily cast. There are alloys in this group suitable for all types of work, including Britannia metal (5 per cent antimony, 3 per cent copper, 92 per cent tin).

Lead

This is a very soft metal which can be scratched with the finger nail. It melts at 327°C and is very malleable, but not ductile, having the lowest tensile strength of the common metals. It dissolves completely in dilute nitric acid, is attacked by concentrated hot sulphuric and hydrochloric acids, but resists them if diluted. It is alloyed with zinc, copper, antimony and other metals for casting and other applications.

Aluminium

Aluminium is one of the most plentiful and widely distributed of all substances. Coming next to oxygen and silicon in the proportion it forms of the earth's crust. It is never found naturally as a native material, but in compositions of slates, clays, shales, schists, and granite rocks. Isolation from its natural composition is complex and although known in the late eighteenth century, it was not separated into the single metallic element on a commercial scale until the latter end of the nineteenth century. It is used for spinning, stamping, forging, and casting in engineering of all types and in the hollow ware and jewellery industries. It is resistant to corrosion due to the formation of a protective oxide layer which can be dyed with vegetable dyes (anodising) to almost any colour and then sealed to form a permanent finish. It melts at approximately 658°C and naturally has a white appearance with a peculiar bluish tinge. It is malleable and ductile. It hardens as other metals, and it can be annealed in the same way, but as it melts before red heat an indicator is required to show the correct annealing temperature. Rub the surface of the metal with soap and when the aluminium has reached the correct temperature the soap turns black. It can be soldered with special solders and fluxes using the soap temperature indicator if necessary. It is readily attacked with a solution of iron perchloride.

Brass

There are a multitude of brasses consisting of the copper and zinc ingredients which may be used in any proportion to produce alloys to suit particular applications. Common yellow brass has them in a 50–50 ratio. Whilst generally hard, and in the case of Delta metal, with almost the tensile strength of steel, most of them remain malleable and ductile, particularly Muntz metal 60–40 brass.

Pinchbeck

A variety of brass named after Christopher Pinchbeck (d 1732) a London clockmaker said to have discovered it. It was used to a large extent in the last century for inexpensive jewellery and watch cases which are now collectors' items. The best pinchbeck consists of 89 per cent copper, 11 per cent zinc to 93 per cent copper and 7 per cent zinc.

Nickel

A white metal with a slight yellowish tinge it easily takes a fine polish. It is one of the hardest and least fusible of metals, being ductile, malleable and tenacious. It melts at approximately 1600°C, may be welded at white heat and welded to iron and certain alloys. Sulphuric and hydrochloric acids have little effect in the cold although it is readily attacked by dilute nitric acid and aqua regia. It has great uses in electro-plating where it can be deposited as an undercoat for other deposits or as a bright surface for machined working surfaces. Electroless nickel is the latest development where the metal is deposited without a current to give a very even decorative surface with remarkable properties as a working surface, often used instead of chrome for areas prone to hard wear and tear. Electro-forming with electroless nickel is highly successful particularly as deposition is much greater than can be achieved electrically.

Nickel Silver

An alloy consisting of 51.6 per cent copper, 25.8 per cent nickel and 22.6 per cent zinc, it has a beautiful bluish-white silver colour, taking on a brilliant polish very easily. Used largely for hollow ware, spoons, forks, candlesticks and jewellery, it is usually plated with silver, gold, or rhodium.

Titanium

This is a light steel-like very hard and tough white metal with a melting point of 1825°C. It can be formed quite easily when hot but is a bit too tough when cold. Although widely distributed it is never found in the native state as a pure metal. It requires expensive complex equipment to extract the pure metal, therefore the cost is quite high. It dissolves in cold dilute sulphuric acid, in hot strong hydrochloric acid and in aqua regia, but less readily in nitric acid. It has to be welded and cast in an argon atmosphere. It may be used as a decorative surface on objects by using the property of the metal to anodise with the formation of an oxide layer, which causes an interference of light, splitting it into the colours of the spectrum. This is achieved by immersing the metal in a solution of sodium chlorate and water and passing a current through it of between 20 and 90 volts; differing colours occur according to the voltage used and length of time applied. Amperage is not critical so the anodising may be carried out with a small 90 volt dry battery. If the titanium is connected to one side of the battery and the metal part of a paint brush connected to the other side, then localised anodising and painting may be carried out by soaking the brush in the sodium chlorate solution and applying it to the metal. This can be very effective and is very easily carried out in the home workshop.

153

Appendix 2

Fahrenheit to Centigrade Conversion

°F to °C—subtract 32 multiply by 5 and divide by 9
°C to °F—multiply by 9 divide by 5 and add 32

Weight Conversion

Grammes to Troy ounces	multiply by 0·0321507
Troy ounces to grammes	multiply by 31·1035

Gauge Comparison Tables

Inch	mm	Birmingham Metal Gauge (Shakespeare's) BMG	Standard Wire Gauge SWG	Approx American B & S
·001	·025	—	50	—
·0012	·030	—	49	—
·0016	·041	—	48	—
·002	·051	—	47	—
·0024	·061	—	46	—
·0028	·071	—	45	—
·0032	·081	—	44	40
·0036	·091	—	43	39
·004	·102	—	42	38
·0044	·112	—	41	37
·0048	·122	—	40	—
·005	·127	—	—	36
·0052	·132	—	39	35
·006	·152	—	38	34
·0065	·165	—	—	—
·0068	·173	—	37	—
·007	·178	—	—	33
·0076	·193	—	36	—
·008	·203	—	—	32
·0084	·213	—	35	—
·0085	·216	1	—	—
·009	·229	—	—	31
·0092	·234	—	34	—
·0095	·241	2	—	—
·010	·254	—	33	30
·0105	·267	3	—	—
·0108	·274	—	32	—
·011	·279	—	—	29

Inch	mm	Birmingham Metal Gauge (Shakespeare's) BMG	Standard Wire Gauge SWG	Approx American B & S
·0116	·295	—	31	—
·012	·305	4	—	—
·0124	·315	—	30	28
·013	·330	—	—	—
·0136	·345	—	29	—
·014	·356	5	—	27
·0148	·376	—	28	—
·015	·381	—	—	—
·016	·406	6	—	—
·0164	·417	—	27	26
·017	·432	—	—	—
·018	·457	—	26	25
·0185	·470	—	—	—
·019	·483	7	—	—
·020	·508	—	25	24
·0215	·546	8	—	—
·022	·559	—	24	23
·024	·610	9	23	—
·025	·635	—	—	22
·027	·686	—	—	—
·028	·711	10	22	21
·030	·762	—	—	—
·032	·813	11	21	20
·033	·838	—	—	—
·035	·889	12	—	—
·036	·914	—	20	19
·038	·965	13	—	—
·039	·991	—	—	—
·040	1.016	—	19	18
·042	1·067	—	—	—
·043	1·092	14	—	—
·046	1·168	—	—	17
·048	1·219	15	18	—
·049	1·244	—	—	—
·051	1·295	16	—	16
·055	1·397	17	—	—
·056	1·422	—	17	—
·058	1·473	—	—	15
·059	1·499	18	—	—
·060	1·524	—	—	—
·062	1·575	19	—	—
·064	1·626	—	16	14
·065	1·651	20	—	—
·067	1·702	—	—	—
·069	1·753	21	—	—
·072	1·829	—	15	13

Inch	mm	Birmingham Metal Gauge (Shakespeare's) BMG	Standard Wire Gauge SWG	Approx American B & S
·073	1·854	22	—	—
·074	1·880	—	—	—
·077	1·956	23	—	—
·080	2·032	—	14	12
·082	2·083	24	—	—
·083	2·108	—	—	—
·086	2·184	—	—	—
·090	2·286	25	—	11
·091	2·311	—	—	—
·092	2·337	—	13	—
·095	2·413	—	—	—
·096	2·438	—	—	—
·100	2·540	26	—	—
·102	2·591	—	—	10
·104	2·642	—	12	—
·109	2·768	—	—	—
·110	2·794	—	—	—
·112	2·845	27	—	9
·116	2·946	—	11	—
·120	3·048	—	—	—
·121	3·073	—	—	—
·124	3·150	28	—	—
·128	3·251	—	10	8
·134	3·403	—	—	—
·136	3·454	29	—	—
·144	3·658	—	9	7
·148	3·759	—	—	—
·150	3·810	30	—	—
·160	4·064	—	8	6
·165	4·191	—	—	—
·166	4·216	31	—	—
·167	4·242	—	—	—
·176	4·470	—	7	—
·180	4·572	—	—	5
·182	4·623	32	—	—
·183	4·648	—	—	—
·192	4·877	—	6	—
·200	5·080	33	—	—
·201	5·105	—	—	—
·203	5·156	—	—	4
·212	5·385	—	5	—
·213	5·410	—	—	—
·216	5·486	34	—	—
·220	5·588	—	—	—
·232	5·893	—	4	3
·238	6·045	35	—	—

Inch	mm	Birmingham Metal Gauge (Shakespeare's) BMG	Standard Wire Gauge SWG	Approx American B & S
·240	6·096	—	—	—
·249	6·325	—	—	—
·250	6·350	36	—	—
·252	6·404	—	3	—
·256	6·502	—	—	2
·259	6·578	—	—	—
·270	6·858	37	—	—
·276	7·010	—	2	—
·278	7·061	38	—	—
·284	7·214	—	—	—
·289	7·341	39	—	1
·300	7·620	40	1	—

Measurement Conversion

Millimetres to inches	multiply by 0·0394
Inches to millimetres	multiply by 25·4

Tempered Steel Heat Colours

	°F	°C	
No colour	200	93	Scrapers
Pale yellow	390	199	
Bright yellow	430	221	
Straw yellow	450	232	Punches, chasing tools
Dark yellow	470	246	
Brownish yellow	480	249	Engraving tools and setting tools
Brownish red	500	260	Hammers, drills
Purple	520	271	
Violet	540	282	
Dark blue	550	288	Cold chisels
Cornflower blue	570	299	Screwdrivers, knives, saws
Bright blue	600	316	Springs
Bluish green/grey	630	332	

Specific Gravities of Metals as applied to Casting

The specific gravity of a metal represents how much heavier a given volume of that metal is compared with the equivalent volume of water. As wax has approximately the same specific gravity as water then the weight of the wax model is multiplied by the specific gravity of the metal in which it is to be cast so as to calculate the gravity of metal required.

Sterling silver	10·46
Gold 22ct	17·70
18ct	15·50
14ct	13·40
10ct	11·57
9ct	11·30
Copper	8·9
Brass	8·5
Bronze	9·0
Tin	7·30
Lead	11·30
Zinc	7·14

Calculating the radius of the disc of metal required for raising a pot from a drawn side elevation (Illus 183)

Draw an accurate side view of the object to be made. Centre line AB and base line CD are drawn in. The elevation is divided into a number of equally spaced lines shown as 1 to 11.

The number is not critical there can be more or less. The length of each of these where they cut through the shape is measured and all added together. This total is then divided by the number of divisions used in this case eleven. This gives the diameter of a parallel sided pot of the same surface area, shown in dotted lines.

Scribe an arc radius EF which cuts base line D at J. Divide GJ to give the radius point H. Scribe an arc about H from G to cut through EF to give point Y. Draw a line from Y to X which is the radius of the disc of metal required to form the original shaped pot.

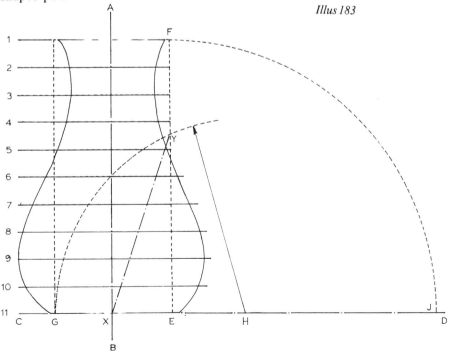

Illus 183

Appendix 3

SUPPLIERS

Bullion Dealers:	Edward, Day & Baker Ltd, 3 Vyse Street, Birmingham 18
	Englehard Sales Ltd, 49 Spencer Street, Birmingham 18 and Valley Road, Cinderford, Gloucester
	Johnson Matthey Ltd, Vittoria Street, Birmingham 1 and 100 High Street, Southgate, London N14 6ET
Casting Equipment:	Hoben Davies Ltd, Spencroft Road, Holditch Industrial Estate, Newcastle-Under-Lyme, Staffs, ST5 9JD
Chemicals:	Bestobell Chemicals, Unit 5, Turriff Warehouse Properties, Station Road, Wolverhampton
Cuttlefish Bone:	Hollywood Pet Supplies, 73 May Lane, Birmingham 47
Decorative Woods:	Hardwoods of Solihull, Thornhill Road, Solihull, West Midlands
Gas Torches:	William Allday & Co Ltd, Alcosa Works, Stourport on Severn, Worcestershire, DY13 9PA
Information:	Gemmological Association of Great Britain, St Dunstans House, Carey Lane, London EC2V 8AB
Ivory, Mother of Pearl, etc:	F. Friedlein & Co Ltd, 718/720 Old Ford Road, London E3 2TA
Jewellers Tools:	F. Meeks Ltd, Warstone Lane, Birmingham 1
	Thomas Sutton Ltd, 37 Frederick Street, Birmingham 18
	H. S. Walsh & E. Gray, 243 Besherham Road, Beckenham, Kent
Laboratory Supplies:	Philip Harris Ltd, Lynn Lane, Shenstone, Staffs, W514 0EE
Lighting:	Herbert Terry & Sons Ltd, Branch Works, Redditch, Worcestershire
Machine Tools:	Hazelwood and Dent Ltd, 89 Barr Street, Birmingham 19
Metal Fabrication	John Lloyd & Sons (Engineers) Ltd,

Lapping Equipment:	12 Frederick Street, Birmingham B1 3HE
Mica:	Birmingham Mica Co Ltd, 3 South Road, Birmingham 18
Non Ferrous Metals:	H. J. Edwards & Sons Ltd, 93 Barr Street, Birmingham 19
	W. Gabb Ltd, 127 Barr Street, Birmingham 19
Polishing, Plating, Lacquers, Chemicals:	W. Canning, Great Hampton Street, Birmingham 18
	Hockley Chemical Co, 1 Hockley Hill, Birmingham 18
Plastics:	Nylonic Engineering Co Ltd, Coppine Side Industrial Estate, Brownhills, Walsall W58 7EX
	P.D.I. Ltd, 33 Hampton Street, Birmingham B19 3LT
Small Equipment:	Buck & Hickman, 23 Whittall Street, Birmingham B4 6DP
	Burnard & Co (Tools) Ltd, 16–18 Vesey Street, Birmingham B4 6JT
	Henri Picard & Frere, Furnival Street, London
Steels and Machine Tools:	T. Norton & Co Ltd, Carver Street, Birmingham B1 3AP
	Uddeholm Ltd, Crown Works, Rubery, Birmingham B45 9AG

Further Reading

CASTING

Bovin, Murray. *Centrifugal or Lost Wax Jewellery Casting* (1973)

Choate, Sharr. *Creative Casting* (Allen & Unwin, 1967)

ENAMELLING

Clarke, Geoffrey and Feher, Francis and Ida. *The Technique of enamelling* (Batsford, 1967)

Neville, Kenneth. *The Craft of Enamelling* (Mills & Boon, 1966)

JEWELLERY MAKING

Bovin, Murray. *Jewelry Making* (1974)

Choate, Sharr. *Creative Gold and Silversmithing* (Allen & Unwin, 1971)

Untracht, Oppi. *Metal Techniques for Craftsmen* (Hale, 1969)

PLASTICS

Clarke, Peter J. *Creative Technology Series* (Allman & Sons, 1971)

——. *Plastics for Schools* (Mills & Boon, 1973)

Kuhnemann, Ursula. *Cold Enamelling*

Zechlin, Katherina. *Setting in Clear Plastics* (Mills & Boon, 1972)

STONES

Wainwright, John. *Discovering Lapidary Work* (Mills & Boon, 1971)

Webster, Robert. *Gemnologists' Compendium* (NAG Press, 1964)

——. *Practical Gemnology* (NAG Press, 1967)

Index